Lord Neaves

The Greek anthology

Lord Neaves

The Greek anthology

ISBN/EAN: 9783337731410

Printed in Europe, USA, Canada, Australia, Japan

Cover: Foto ©ninafisch / pixelio.de

More available books at **www.hansebooks.com**

THE
GREEK ANTHOLOGY

BY

LORD NEAVES

ONE OF THE SENATORS OF THE COLLEGE OF JUSTICE
IN SCOTLAND

PHILADELPHIA
J. B. LIPPINCOTT & CO.
1875.

CONTENTS.

		PAGE
CHAP. I.	INTRODUCTION,	1
" II.	DEDICATORY,	17
" III.	SEPULCHRAL,	57
" IV.	AMATORY,	80
" V.	DIDACTIC,	97
" VI.	LITERARY AND ARTISTIC,	118
" VII.	WITTY AND SATIRICAL,	179
" VIII.	NARRATIVE AND MISCELLANEOUS,	197

THE GREEK ANTHOLOGY.

CHAPTER I.

INTRODUCTION.

THE Collection, or rather the Collections, of small poems known as the Greek "Anthology," have long been an object of great interest to scholars. They have been much studied and repeatedly edited. The individual poems, or selections from them, have been often translated and often imitated. They employed the best care of the great printer, Henry Stephens. They were favourite subjects of study with Erasmus, and his friend Sir Thomas More. The greater part of them were excellently translated into Latin verse by Hugo Grotius, a man sometimes overrated and sometimes underrated, but undoubtedly eminent in various departments of learning—as a scholar, a jurist, and a theologian. The poet Gray, a critic of nice and fastidious taste, made them the object of particular attention, and enriched an interleaved copy of Stephens's Anthology with copious notes, parallel passages, and conjectural emendations, besides transfusing several of the epigrams into Latin verse. They beguiled some of the weary hours which Johnson felt heavy on his hands in his last illness, and they helped to cheer the melancholy and morbid life which was the lot of the amiable Cowper.

It is true that, amidst the general chorus of approbation which they have excited, a few *anserine* discords have occasionally been heard. Chesterfield, in his famous Letters, thus peremptorily denounces them to his son: "I hope you will keep company with Horace and Cicero among the Romans, and Homer and Xenophon among the Greeks, and that you have got out of the worst company in the world—the Greek epigrams. Martial has wit, and is worth looking into sometimes; but I recommend the Greek epigrams to your supreme contempt." But whatever we may think of his lordship in respect of knowledge of life and worldly wisdom, we are not disposed to bow to his authority in literature any more than in morals.

The supposed insipidity of Greek epigrams had been a well-known subject of jest in Paris in the century preceding Chesterfield's time. Racan, the French poet, was shown by a lady some epigrams of her own composition. He pronounced them *bad*, because they wanted point. She replied that that was of no consequence, as they were epigrams *à la Grecque*. They met at dinner soon afterwards, where the soup served up was not very palatable, and the lady observed to Racan that it was abominable. He replied: "Mademoiselle, it is *soupe à la Grecque*," which expression having got abroad became a favourite mode of designating an indifferent soup.* A French poet, or indeed a French man of fashion generally, was likely enough to miss in the Greek compositions the piquancy for which his own literature is so remarkable, and Chesterfield's school of taste was eminently French. But Menage himself, who tells the story given above, but who was a good scholar, and a considerable wit, appreciated highly the Greek epigrams, and composed a good many Greek imitations of them.

Men of the greatest learning and best taste have, since Chesterfield's time and down to our own day, given a very different verdict from his opinion, and, we may say, have done so unanimously. We find, no doubt, in the Anthology, that admixture of good, bad, and indifferent which Martial pronounces to be unavoidable in all similar collections; but to prefer Martial to his Greek prototypes, or rather predecessors, as Chesterfield does, would now be universally held to be blind and tasteless criticism. We feel assured that, even under the disadvantages arising from their wearing an English dress, the specimens given in this volume will justify to its readers the high estimate of the Anthology which has so completely gained the ascendant among men of true discernment.

Until the beginning of the seventeenth century the only "Greek Anthology" considered to be extant in anything like a complete state was the collection made

* Menagiana, 165.

by Maximus Planudes, a monk of Constantinople, who flourished about the middle or in the earlier half of the fourteenth century. Planudes was considered to have compiled this collection from an Anthology, or, as it was called, a "Cycle," of epigrams, put together by Agathias—surnamed, from his study of law, Scholasticus—a well-known though heavy historian, who was a native of Myrinè, and lived in the time of Justinian, in the sixth century after Christ. Planudes's collection was distributed into seven books, under different heads, according to the subjects treated of.

It was about the year 1606 that the great scholar Salmasius, then a youth of eighteen, discovered in the library of the Palatinate at Heidelberg another MS. of a Greek Anthology, compiled by Constantinus Cephalas, of whom not even the name had been previously heard. Cephalas appears to have lived about the beginning of the tenth century, and thus, in point of chronology, occupies an intermediate position between Agathias and Planudes. The latter collector, as seems now to be probable, employed himself chiefly in abridging and rearranging the work of Cephalas, which is generally the more copious of the two, though not on all subjects. Planudes has been somewhat harshly assailed as not merely destitute of taste, but as having expurgated lines and even stanzas in the original poems, and either omitted them altogether or replaced them with phraseology of his own. We are not willing, however, to cancel or much diminish the debt which we undoubtedly owe him; and there are not a few epigrams suppressed by him which have since come to light, and which had better never have been published or never written. His Anthology, until Salmasius's discovery, was the only considerable repertory of this kind of literature, and was a source of inexhaustible interest, amusement, and instruction to many generations of scholars. Planudes, though his taste may have been defective, was a man of learning as well as of worth. He translated into Greek Ovid's Metamorphoses and other Latin works; and it seems now to be proved that he was not the author of a foolish life of Æsop that was long ascribed to him.

It is remarkable that while the Palatine Anthology had been discovered by Salmasius so early as the beginning of the seventeenth century, and the discovery made generally known, and although it was the declared intention of Salmasius to publish it immediately, a number of circumstances interfered for a long time to prevent that step being taken; and it was only about the end of the last or the beginning of the present century, at an interval of nearly two hundred years, that it was given to the world by Brunck and by Jacobs. The MS. had in the mean time gone through a variety of adventures, having been removed to the Vatican in 1623 with the rest of the Palatine library, thereafter transferred to Paris in 1797, and in 1815 finally restored to Heidelberg, where we suppose it now lies, if none of the recent German arrangements have led to a change.

Partial transcripts of it had in the mean time been made, but the final publication of the Palatine manuscript, and the attention and careful study which it called forth from German scholars, who generally do thoroughly whatever they undertake, threw a great deal of additional light on this branch of literature. These studies, pursued with much ardour by various scholars, have in a special manner brought into conspicuous notice the name of Meleager, the first and most considerable of the *flower-gatherers*, for such is the English equivalent for the word "anthologist." He was a Syrian, and flourished in the early part of the century preceding the commencement of our era. He collected the fragments of Greek poetry and genius which before his time were either intrusted to the memories of men, engraven on marbles or other solid structures, or dispersed in miscellaneous works as fugitive pieces. These he named his "Garland," and prefixed to it, as a preface or *prœmium*, a set of verses extending to nearly 60 lines, in which he characterises each or the principal part of the writers included in his collection by a flower or plant emblematical of his or her peculiar genius. But Meleager was not merely a collector, he was also a composer, of epigrams, and his compositions may take a high place in comparison with the average or all but the best of those inserted in his "Garland." His character seems to have been a remarkable one, not free from great faults, ardent in his passions, and acute in his susceptibilities, but with a high idea of the dignity of the poet's art, and a lively and just appreciation of the Beautiful. Another collector after Meleager was Philippus of Thessalonica, who lived in the time of Trajan, and who also contributed some original epigrams and prefixed a proem to his collection. Finally, there came Agathias, already mentioned, the last of the ancient anthologists, whose collection was entitled a "Cycle" or Circle of poetical compositions, and who himself, like his predecessors, contributed some original epigrams, not indeed equal to those of Meleager, but yet not destitute of taste and elegance. Contributions to his collection were also supplied by his contemporary and friend, Paul the Silentiary, who at the court of Justinian held an office in some degree corresponding to that of Gentleman usher.

Generally speaking, the space of time over which the writers of the Greek epigrams successively flourished may be said to extend to upwards of a thousand years—from Simonides, if we call him the earliest, down to Agathias as the latest of them—a period, undoubtedly, of very long duration for a language and literature to retain such a wonderful vitality, and, amidst some fallings off, a certain similarity of style and character. It might be doubted if some of the latest of these writers deserved the name of Classical in the highest sense of the term. But Agathias, the last in the list, has so well caught the ancient spirit, that it would be harsh to exclude him. After his era the degeneracy of the literature became unmistakable.

None of these more ancient collections descended entire to modern times, and we know them mainly in the compilations formed from them successively by Cephalas and by Planudes. The name of "Anthology" is still employed on the same principle on which Meleager originally regarded his collections as wreaths or gar lands, the poems composing it being assimilated to flowers of varied kinds and hues. The individual poems have been called Epigrams, a term which originally and literally denoted simply an Inscription, though the word was in process of time transferred to a different class of compositions—and perhaps it might have been convenient to have two words, *epigram* and *epigraph*, to note the distinction.

The tendencies of the Greek mind in originally building up this species of literature are well explained by Jacobs, the ablest and the most diligent of the editors of the Anthologies. He speaks of the ancient Greeks as the most religious of men; using the epithet, as we conceive, in a favourable sense, to designate that feeling of dependence and gratitude towards divine power which, however alloyed by a mixture of superstition and a leaning to sensuous forms of worship, had in it much of the essence of a true piety. In this spirit he tells us that, referring to the gods all events, whether prosperous or adverse, they were accustomed, when their wars had been successfully concluded and their enemies subdued, to set apart a portion of their booty or of its profits to the honour of those deities to whose protection they thought that they owed the victory, as well as to dedicate to them in their temples and shrines the arms of which their enemies were stripped. This, he considers, was the oldest form of offerings and inscriptions, and others of an analogous kind were gradually added. Prizes won in public games, or some equivalent for them, were dedicated by the victors to the gods who patronised them. The old soldier consecrated the weapons and armour he was no longer fit or likely to use. Mechanics and labourers did so in like manner with the implements of their industry, when these were worn out, or when the owners changed their own employments. Even playthings, when laid aside, were thus dedicated, a common feeling of affectionate remembrance prompting the owners to place them under the protection of a temple, rather than leave them exposed to the rude accidents of chance or neglect. Moral sentences came to be put up as inscriptions on statues or memorial columns; and we read of a desire shown by the Pisistratidæ to disseminate in this way prudential maxims or impressive truths by inscribing them in verse upon the Hermæ, or busts of Mercury, which formed their milestones or landmarks. It is needless to say that inscriptions on tombs were a natural and obvious mode of preserving the memory of the dead and recording the affection of the living.

The workings of the Greek character, as tending in these many ways to embody and perpetuate the national feeling of rude and sometimes, as it almost seems, of infantine piety, are nowhere better analysed and described than in those well-known passages in Wordsworth's "Excursion" which it is unnecessary to quote, where he deals with the genesis of natural religion in different countries and under different circumstances. These feelings, as Wordsworth shows in a continuation of the same passage, led them to look at the more beautiful or striking scenes of nature and natural objects as animated by some spiritual essence that could be reverenced and addressed, and hence their affectionate consecration of their rivers, hills, and groves to the deities or semi-deities under whose care they seemed to be placed.

> "'Take, running river, take these locks of mine,'
> Thus would the Votary say—'this severed hair,
> My vow fulfilling, do I here present,
> Thankful for my belovèd child's return.'"

All of these impulses are exhibited in the poems of the Anthology, which thus acquire an additional interest from the light they throw upon the manners, customs, and beliefs of this remarkable people. The wide range of topics embraced in the anthologies has been well depicted by De Bosch in some Latin lines to the memory of Grotius, printed in his edition of the Anthology, in which Grotius's translations first appeared, and which we venture thus to render in some of its most striking parts:—

> Whoe'er delights in themes from history's page,
> These varied studies will his thirst assuage;
> Here sacred bards their liberal aid bestow
> The fates of gods and goddesses to show;
> Wisdom may sometimes wear a look austere,
> But smiles and jests are oft her helpmates here;
> Venus and every Grace for victory vie,
> And fast the Idalian darts of Cupid fly.
> By disc or javelin now the prize is won,
> On horseback or on foot the race is run.
> The graceful Muse has here concisely sung
> The charms that woman sends from eye or tongue;

What men have done she gives to understand,
Whose zeal has saved or raised their native land.

. . . .

Cities, that in the dust long buried lie,
Rear in their ancient seats their heads on high.
Traces of shrines and temples seem to stand
Heaped with large gifts from many a pious hand.
The sad laments of friends now strike our ears;
Our eyes now see the child's, the parent's tears.
We hear the widow's wail, when doomed to mourn
A loved one lost, and clasp his lifeless urn.
Lessons of wisdom open to our view
In all life's varied scenes of gay or gloomy hue.

The inscriptions that existed in Greece were innumerable. Even those that still remain, either in their original sites or removed to munificent libraries or museums, are very numerous, and we have the terms of many more preserved in ancient books. But it is not every epigram that can claim a place in an Anthology. It must for that purpose be an *anthos* or flower, possessing an attraction from some beauty or elegance, from some ingenuity or elevation of sentiment. Many inscriptions of great historical interest are thus excluded. It is interesting to read in Plutarch of the pillar that Theseus is said to have erected on the Isthmus of Corinth to mark the boundary between Attica and the Peloponnesus. On one side of it were the words, "This is not Peloponnesus, but Ionia;" on the other, "This is Peloponnesus, not Ionia;"— of which ancient inscription an imitation was put up on Hadrian's arch at Athens, dividing the older town from the part that the Roman emperor had renovated :—

> "This Athens is the primitive town of Theseus.
> This is the town of Adrian, not of Theseus."

Still more interesting is it to read the very words of that inscription to which Milton so touchingly refers in his sonnet, beginning, " Captain or colonel, or knight in arms "—when he entreats that his " defenceless doors " may be preserved from harm amidst the civil disturbances :—

> "Lift not thy spear against the Muses' bower:
> The great Emathian Conqueror bid spare
> The house of Pindarus, when temple and tower
> Went to the ground."

The actual inscription by which Alexander the Great preserved Pindar's house, when Thebes was given over to be sacked by his soldiers, has been preserved by some ancient antiquaries, and runs thus :—

> "Of Pindarus the poet do not burn the house."

Again, on the base of the wonderful statue of Olympian Jove, the name of the sculptor was thus inscribed in an hexameter line, at what time does not appear :—

> "Phidias, Charmides' son, the Athenian citizen, made ME."

A startling inscription, and involving a strange mixture of ideas! The statue is made to speak as a person, and thus almost becomes the god himself, and yet this god describes the artist as having *made* him. How difficult to reconcile this fact with what is told of Stilpo the philosopher, that he was banished by the Areopagus for saying that the Minerva in the Citadel of Athens was no divinity, but the work of Phidias the sculptor! But interesting as these inscriptions are, they do not belong to an anthology. Even those of them that have a metrical form are too much mere matter-of-fact to have a place in a Garland.

It should here be added that the parentage of individual epigrams is often very uncertain. We know generally what poets had places in Meleager's and Philippus's collections, from the enumeration of their names in the proems. But we are still in doubt as to the individual poems which they wrote, and often there are a variety of persons of the same name who wrote poems not easily distinguishable. In this perplexity we are often driven to resort to internal evidence, which is not always a safe guide, though on the whole it may keep us from any great blunder. In general, the simpler and more natural the composition is, if it has genius at all, the more likely it is to be an ancient and original inscription.

The Greek Anthology, therefore, in its largest sense —swelled as it has been by contributions from various sources — may now be considered as consisting, not merely of the collections of Cephalas and Planudes, but also of a large number of other short poems deserving the name of epigrams or epigraphs, found scattered about among the old Greek historians, biographers, and miscellaneous writers, and which it is likely that Meleager, Philippus, or Agathias, if we had them entire, would be found to have inserted in their collections, or might reasonably have done so. But the longer and more elaborate compositions, not of an inscriptional character, ought perhaps to be excluded from this class, though it is not always easy to draw the line, and most of the modern editors of the Greek Anthology have occasionally overstepped the limit.

We have already indicated that the primitive Greek epigram differs much from the modern idea attached to the word. From the time of Martial, indeed, the epigram came to be characterised generally by that peculiar *point* or sting, which we now look for in a French or English epigram; and the want of this in the old Greek compositions doubtless led some minds to think them tame and tasteless. The true or the best form of the early Greek epigram does not aim at wit or seek to produce surprise. Its purpose is to set forth in the shortest, simplest, and plainest language, but yet with perfect purity and even elegance of diction, some fact or feeling of such interest as would prompt the real or supposed speaker to record it in the form of an epigram; though it is true that, particularly in the later period of epigrammatic writing, these compositions, even among the Greeks, assumed a greater variety of aspect, and were employed as the vehicle of satire or ridicule, as a means of producing hilarity and mirth. A good many of the epigrammatists flourished in or after the age of Martial, and may have followed or co-operated with him to produce this change of style.

It seems of great importance at the present time to recall attention to these early monuments of genius and taste. They are highly characteristic of the Greek mind, which in those compositions that did not deal with fervid or majestic expression, looked to the combination of perfect simplicity with perfect beauty as their true ideal; and this, in great things or in little, in sculpture or in poetry, in the statue that enchants the world or the epigraph that in a few lines has power to touch the heart or please the fancy. Much of these excellences, particularly of diction, must be lost in translation, as the structure of the classical languages, especially the Greek, afforded facilities for condensation and elegance unattainable in English. Even the attempt, however, to imitate this character, may help to purify the taste, in an age when the poet is not always free from obscurity, when the art of concealing art seems not often practised, when condensation is not thought of, and simplicity is considered to be insipidity.

The first serious attempt to exhibit the true character of the Greek epigram in English translation was in the papers which appeared in 'Blackwood's Magazine' in the years 1833 and 1834, from the pen of Professor Wilson, assisted by many friends, and particularly by Mr William Hay, who for some years devoted much of his scholarship and powers of versification to this task. The effort thus made was eminently successful, and has tended very much to throw into the shade the more vague and diffuse versions which had proceeded from previous translators, including even Elton, and Bland and Merivale, to whom, however, we owe a deep debt of gratitude for doing so much to revive, in the present century, a taste for this species of poetry.

It is not easy to determine in what order compositions of this kind should be treated. On the whole, it seems best not to deal with them chronologically, or even according to the authors to whom they are attributed, which is often a matter of difficulty, in consequence of the authorship being doubtful. It seems a preferable course to divide them into classes, and in this way to keep together epigrams of the same character, which will facilitate comparison. The classes into which we shall divide them are these : 1, Dedicatory ; 2, Sepulchral ; 3, Amatory ; 4, Didactic ; 5, Literary and Artistic ; 6, Witty and Satirical ; 7, Narrative and Miscellaneous.

CHAPTER II.

DEDICATORY.

WE proceed to give select specimens of epigrams, beginning with the class that may be called Dedicatory or Votive. These all involve the common idea that something is consecrated or offered up to some divine power; and it is thought that under this division may be, and ought properly to be introduced, among other varieties, the monumental records of victories and remarkable public events, where the monument is truly considered as made sacred by the greatness of the subject, and by the intention thereby to show gratitude to the gods for benefits received.

Ranging as these epigrams do over so great a portion of time, there is one feature in which they may materially differ from each other. Some of them have been actual inscriptions, while others are mere literary exercises or compositions of such a kind as might be appropriately inscribed to celebrate any memorable achievement or occurrence. These diversities in the epigrams will necessarily tell upon their internal character, for in an actual inscription the poet may dispense with any detail as to those things that are patent to the eye. The reader of such an epigram or epigraph on the spot, does not need to be told where it is erected, or on what material it is inscribed; he has merely to learn the subject, the occasion, and the author or orderer of the inscription. But an epigram that is a mere literary production, while it does all this, must also do more, and tell the reader something as to the place and position in which the imaginary inscription is to be supposed to have been put up.

Of these two kinds of epigram it is needless to say that the first is the more ancient, and will also in general be found to be the shorter, the simpler, and the more direct of the two. Some critics think that the fictitious, or imaginary inscription, was not known or practised before the time of Alexander the Great; but be that as it may, the real inscription, of which many specimens have been preserved, is certainly more interesting and valuable, as it also is, generally speaking, more vigorous and lifelike, than the other kind.

Of the composers of ancient epigrams that were actual epigraphs, the most remarkable is Simonides of Ceos, particularly if we look to the number as well as to the merit of his compositions. His birth is placed, by Clinton, in the year 556 B.C., and his death in 467, in the 90th year of his age. He is the same to whom Wordsworth refers in those beautiful lines:—

> "O ye, who patiently explore
> The wreck of Herculanean lore,
>   What rapture could ye seize
> Some Theban fragment, or unroll
> One precious tender-hearted scroll
>   Of pure Simonides!"

Some of the pieces bearing the name of this author may be the productions of other and inferior artists; for three of the name, at least, attained distinction as poets, and the family had a professional and hereditary connection with poetry and musical representation. In the great Simonides the fire of patriotism, or at least the power of expressing it, burned with so bright a glow, that it is difficult to mistake his compositions on such subjects. But they are also distinguished by much simplicity and compression, as well as by great sobriety and purity of thought. "When young," we are told in Dr Smith's Biography, "he formed a part of the brilliant literary circle which Hipparchus collected at his court. In advanced life he enjoyed the personal friendship of Themistocles and Pausanias, and celebrated their exploits: and in his extreme old age he found an honoured retreat at the court of Syracuse." The residence of Simonides at Syracuse is particularly memorable for two things. It was he who, as Cicero tells us in his 'Nature of the Gods,' was asked by Hiero who or what God was, when he requested a day's time to think of his answer. On subsequent days he always doubled the period required for deliberation; and when Hiero inquired the reason, he replied that the longer he considered the subject, the more obscure it appeared. The other circumstance to which we refer is, that Xenophon in his 'Hiero' introduces him as the person to whom the Sicilian tyrant unbosoms himself as to the miseries and dangers of that "bad eminence." On turning to the volume on

Xenophon in this series, our readers will be able to judge of the estimation in which Simonides must have been held for sagacity and wisdom. He seems to have been the first inventor of what is called Mnemonics, or the science of Artificial Memory.

Two events are mentioned as having occurred to Simonides, which have rather a fabulous air. It is said that having given burial to a dead body which lay exposed on the sea-shore — an act which was held among the Greeks to be an indispensable duty of humanity — the dead man appeared to him in a dream, and warned him not to go on board of a certain vessel in which he had intended to sail, and that by following this advice his life was saved, as the vessel was lost on her voyage.

On this subject an epigram is preserved, which runs thus, having reference to some supposed representation of his dream:—

"The Saviour of Simonides, the Ceian, here you see,
Who, dead, repaid the living man—an act of piety."

His life was again saved on another occasion in this way. He had written a eulogistic poem upon the Thessalian prince, Scopas, for which he was to receive a certain remuneration. He had introduced into the poem, also, some laudatory verses on the Dioscuri (Castor and Pollux), and Scopas, on settling the transaction, refused to pay him more than a half of the stipulated sum, telling him to apply to the Dioscuri for the other half. Soon afterwards, when Simonides was present in the house of Scopas, he was told that two young men wished to speak with him, and going to the door he saw no one; but while gazing around him in astonishment, the house which he had just left fell, and killed Scopas and the other guests, while Simonides was saved.

As already mentioned, Simonides was a professional poet, and, as Bentley irreverently says, one of "a string," including Pindar, that got their livelihood by the Muses. It is certain that he would be largely remunerated from the public treasury for his historical epigrams, just as the Italian poet Sannazaro got from the Venetian Senate 600 ducats for his epigram of six lines on the beauty of Venice. But it may be inferred, from their brevity and condensation, that the payment of Simonides would be measured rather by the merits than by the length of his compositions.

Many of his short poems were written in celebration of victories gained at the public games of Greece, and for these, no doubt, he would also be liberally paid. Aristotle tells a story of him, that upon being asked to celebrate for a trifling remuneration a victory gained in a mule-race, he declined, upon the ground that it was beneath the dignity of the Muse to praise the offspring of an ass; but that, upon the terms being increased, he dignified the subjects of his song by designating the mules as the daughters of "storm-footed steeds;" choosing thus to elevate them by a reference to their generous mothers, rather than to degrade them by speaking of their ignoble sires.

One of the earliest of the epigrams made by Simonides upon a public event had reference to the erection of an image of the god Pan in connection with the battle of Marathon.

The circumstances which gave rise to this event are these: The Athenians, when they marched towards Marathon to meet the enemy, sent off a messenger of noted speed to require instant succour from Sparta. The Athenian courier, as Thirlwall tells the story, travelling with breathless haste, reached Sparta the next day after he had left Athens. The Spartans did not refuse assistance; but they did not feel the urgency of the juncture, and dismissed the messenger with promises of distant succour. On rejoining his fellow-citizens, he announced to them assurances of aid from an invisible hand. As he crossed the top of the mountains that separate Argolis from Arcadia, the god Pan, he said, had called him by his name, and had bidden him cheer the Athenians with a gracious reproach for having neglected the worship of a deity who had often befriended them in time past, and would prove his goodwill toward them yet again. In reference to these occurrences, and in allusion to the panic which he was supposed to have created in the Persian army, the statue of Pan seems to have been erected by Miltiades, for which the epigram by Simonides was written.

The closest translation we can find is here given, being confined, as the original is, to a single couplet:—

"Me, goat-foot Pan, the Arcad—the Medes' fear,
The Athenians' friend—Miltiades placed here."

It will be noticed that, with all its brevity, this epigram states every circumstance necessary to make the story intelligible. The name of the god is given, and his deformed aspect is mentioned as the means by which he was the better able to strike terror where he wished to do so. His country of Arcadia is named, as enlisting his sympathies in behalf of Greece; his enmity to the Medes, and his friendship for the Athenians, are celebrated, as having led to the erection of his statue; and, finally, the name of the general is recorded by whom the dedication was made.

A still more celebrated epigram by Simonides refers to the battle of Thermopylæ; and it is a striking fact that the same poet who, when an elderly man, had celebrated the victory at Marathon, the first struggle with the Persians, should be called upon ten years afterwards, and should still retain sufficient poetical power, to record the chief events of the second Persian invasion. The epigram to which we refer has been often translated. There are eighteen English versions of it in the article on the Anthology in 'Blackwood's Magazine,'* all of them good, but we select the version by Bowles, which Christopher North there says is the best, "and is perfect." The epigram, it will be seen, has a special reference to the Spartans who fell at Thermopylæ along with their king, Leonidas, whose march to that place was impelled probably by a feeling in their government that as Athens had gained the victory at Marathon without assistance from the Pelo-

* Vol. xxxiv. p. 970.

ponnesus, it was now Sparta's turn to take the lead. This is the epigram :—

> "Go tell the Spartans, thou that passest by,
> That here, obedient to their laws, we lie."

There happens to be a various reading in the second line of the Greek, which makes it doubtful whether the expression used was "laws" or "words." Cicero, who translated the epigram, seems to have read "laws;" but the idea is the same, as either term was probably intended to indicate the institutions of Sparta.

Christopher North says as to this noble epigram: "'Tis but two lines, and all Greece for centuries had them by heart. She forgot them, and Greece was living Greece no more." The lines indeed, simple as they are, contain the very essence of those elements which go to make military virtue and patriotic fidelity. We do not underrate the love of glory or the sense of honour in war, or in public service of any kind. We may admire that class of warriors whom the English poet thus addresses :—

> "On, ye brave,
> Who rush to glory, or the grave!"

But these are not the highest feelings that should enter into a soldier's career. Obedience to lawful supreme command is the life-blood of military virtue; and this epigram, as well as the noble act which it records, illustrates that truth. The combatants at Thermopylæ are not made to boast of their courage; what they ask the passer-by to announce at home is, that they lie there *in obedience* to the laws or commands of their countrymen. They were sent out to stand in the gap in defence of Greece against the myriads of Asia, and were bid to die rather than retreat. They did so, and that is the simple report which they wish to be conveyed to Sparta. The effect of what they did corresponded with the virtue which the deed displayed, by shaking the confidence of the enemy and animating Greek courage, not only at the time, and during that crisis, but in subsequent and similar dangers in after-ages. This virtue of obedience, it is thought, is the great distinction which gives pre-eminence to one military nation over another. If we find that of two nations, one has its fighting men animated mainly by a love of glory, and the other mainly by a sense of duty, we may easily predict on which side the ultimate victory will be. In the two greatest warriors of the present century, the sense of duty was the paramount feeling, both in their own minds, and as impressed by them upon their followers. Neither of them can have been indifferent to fame, but duty is what they both preached and practised. On the last day of Nelson's life, and, we may add, the last day (for the time) of the existence of a French navy, the watchword for the fight reminded the Fleet of what was expected of the men,—to do their duty; that was all, but that was enough. Nelson fell, while England had the reward of victory. It is this simple rule which prompts the exertions of the true soldier, described in Wolfe's favourite song as one " whose business 'tis to die." This Spartan obedience, which

Simonides long ago celebrated, is that virtue which will in all times gain the ascendant both in war and in peace.

The number of Spartans at Thermopylæ is generally said to have been three hundred, exclusive of the Helots; and the total number of Greeks accompanying the Spartans would be a few thousands. The disparity between this handful and the number of the Persians was sufficiently great to give rise to the following simple but expressive epigram, which is to be found recorded in Herodotus, and which is also ascribed to Simonides:—

"Four thousand men Peloponnesus brought,
Who 'gainst three hundred myriads nobly fought."

The chief epigram that we have given in connection with Thermopylæ has reference to men who had fallen in the battle. But this does not make the composition an ordinary epitaph. Its tone is not mournful, but triumphant. It is not a dirge, but a pæan appropriate to the death of heroes, of that little "remnant of the Greeks," who, as Thirlwall describes them, "armed only with a few swords, stood a butt for the arrows, the javelins, and the stones of the enemy, which at length overwhelmed them. Where they fell they were afterwards buried; their tomb, as Simonides sings, was an altar, a sanctuary in which Greece revered the memory of her second founders." The language of Simonides, here referred to, occurs in the fragment of a hymn to the Spartans who fell at Thermopylæ, and may be thus translated:—

"Of those at famed Thermopylæ who lie,
Glorious the fortune, bright the destiny.
Their tomb an altar is; their noble name
A fond remembrance of ancestral fame.
Their death, a song of triumph; neither rust
Nor time, that turns all mortal things to dust,
Shall dim the splendour of that holy shrine,
Where Greece for ever sees her native virtues shine."

These epigrams, on the Spartans generally, were by public authority inscribed on pillars in their honour; while another epigram is also mentioned by Herodotus as an individual tribute to Megistias, a noble-hearted Spartan, whose sagacity had gained him the reputation of a prophet. Being in the camp at Thermopylæ with Leonidas, and both of them being certain of the impending fate of the Grecian force there assembled, Leonidas gave him his dismissal, that they might not both perish. Megistias, however, refused to go, but sent away his only son, who was serving with him in the army. He himself perished in the fight, and Herodotus expressly tells us that Simonides made this epigram upon the soothsayer in consequence of the relation of hospitality existing between them:—

"Of famed Megistias here behold the tomb,
  Slain by the Medes who crossed Sperchèus' tide:
A Seer, who well foresaw his coming doom,
  But would not leave his Spartan leader's side."

The name of Themistocles is so much identified with the final defeat of the Persian invaders, that those epigrams which relate to him appear appropriately to come under consideration at this place. His life and fate afford a strange proof of the inconsistencies of human character, or of the inconstancy of popular feeling. Notwithstanding the boundless benefits which he had conferred upon Athens, his countrymen proved ungrateful; though that ingratitude might find some excuse in his own imprudence in boasting of his conduct, and ostentatiously asserting his merits, as well as in some delinquencies by which he was said to have derived benefit from his public administration. He was at last condemned to exile, and, strange to say, found refuge at the court of Persia, where a pension was conferred upon him, and the town of Magnesia assigned him as a residence. He obtained these favours apparently by promising to produce some plan for aggrandising the Persians at the expense of his own country. But whether in this he was playing false with the barbarians, or really entertained unpatriotic designs against Greece, seems to be a matter on which different opinions may prevail. At his death a splendid monument was raised to him in the public place of Magnesia, but a tomb was also pointed out in the Piræus at Athens, to which his bones were supposed to have been privately conveyed.

However splendid in other respects his tomb at Magnesia might be, it was not likely to set forth his achievements against the Persians, within whose territory it lay. The following epigram was composed as if to supply this defect, and is attributed to Philippus the Anthologist:—

"Trace on my tomb the mountains and the sea,
And let the all-seeing Sun a witness be:

Trace, too, the streams, whose deep and copious course
Xerxes dried up with his unnumbered force.
Add Salamis; and make the shrine, that stands
Reared to my memory by Magnesian hands,
Such as Themistocles' high fame demands."

Another by Geminus, in the same style, begins with these words:—

" Give me no grave but Greece ;"

but afterwards proceeds much as that of Philippus does: though it would appear that Philippus here was the plagiarist.

A few more epigrams by different authors will dismiss the subject of Greek history as far as it seems necessary to dwell upon it here. Several of these bear the name of Simonides, but a reference to the chronology of the events which they commemorate shows that they must be referred to a younger relative of the name.

The first relates to the double victory gained by the Athenian general Cimon over the Persians on the same day both by sea and land, an event which happened in the year following that in which Simonides is said to have died. The translation we give is by Merivale:—

' Ne'er since that olden time when Asia stood
First torn from Europe by the ocean flood,
Since horrid Mars first poured on either shore
The storm of battle and its wild uproar,
Hath man by land and sea such glory won,
As for the mighty deed this day was done.

> By land, the Medes in myriads press the ground ;
> By sea, a hundred Tyrian ships are drowned,
> With all their martial host ; while Asia stands
> Deep groaning by, and wrings her helpless hands."

This double victory is the event to which Pope satirically alludes in the " Dunciad," by comparing to it a Lord Mayor's procession by land and water :—

> " 'Twas on the day when . . . rich and grave,
> Like Cimon, triumphed both on land and wave."

The next epigram, also translated by Merivale, relates to the same day's events, and may probably be ascribed in like manner to the younger Simonides.

On Those who Fell at the Eurymedon.

> " These by the streams of famed Eurymedon,
> Their envied youth's short brilliant race have run ·
> In swift-winged ships, and on the embattled field,
> Alike they forced the Median bows to yield,
> Breaking their foremost ranks. Now here they lie,
> Their names inscribed on rolls of victory."

A few more epigrams may here be given upon Marathon and Thermopylæ, and the Persian invasion generally. The first is by *the* Simonides, the rest by miscellaneous writers :—

> " Nobly to die ! if that be virtue's crown,
> Fortune to us her bounty well displayed.
> · Striving to make Greece free, we gained renown
> That shrouds us where we lie, and ne'er can fade."

> " These to their country brought an endless name,
> When death's dark cloud around themselves they drew ;
> Nor dying, did they die : their virtue's fame
> From Hades brings them back to live anew."

The next epigram that we come to appears in two forms; in one as a single couplet, in another as consisting of an addition that extends it to six lines. The first couplet may be enough to give. The peculiar phrase in the first line corresponds to a Greek proverbial expression used to denote any crisis or important turning-point in human affairs.

" When on a razor's edge all Hellas stood,
We, who lie here, preserved her with our blood.

The epigram that follows has reference to the victory gained over the Persians at Platæa, on which occasion the lines are said to have been inscribed on the altar of the Eleutherian Jove (Jove the deliverer), near to which solemn sacrifices in honour of that deity were for a long time periodically offered up.

" Here, when the Greeks, by strength of heart and hand,
Had driven the Persians from the Hellenic land,
A record of delivered Greece to prove,
They raised this shrine to the Deliverer, Jove."

This is an inscription for a trophy in the temple of Minerva, obviously referable to the Persian war; the translation is from Bland's collection:—

" From wounds and death they rest—this bow and quiver,
Beneath Minerva's holy roof for ever:
Once did their shafts along the battle speed,
And drink the life-blood of the charging Mede."

This is by an unknown author:—

" Miltiades, the Persians all thy warlike prowess found,
And by thy virtue, Marathon is consecrated ground."

This is by Parmenio, in reference to Xerxes' marvellous exertions :—

"Him who reversed the laws that Nature gave,
Sailed o'er the land, and walked upon the wave,
Mars, with three hundred spears from Sparta's plain,
Arrested: blush, ye mountains, and thou main!"

This also is ascribed to Simonides, and is said to be on the Corinthians who fell at Salamis :—

"Well-watered Corinth was our home before;
We lie on Salamis' Aiantian shore.
The ships of Tyre, the Persian, and the Mede
We routed, and thus holy Greece we freed."

What follows next is a singular epigram, also by Simonides, referring to supplications offered up to Venus by her Corinthian votaries for the safety of Greece against the Persian invasion; in remembrance of which, at the end of the war, the Corinthians are said to have dedicated to the goddess a painted tablet :—

"These divine women to fair Venus prayed
To give the struggling friends of Greece her aid;
And She the Greek Acropolis decreed
Not to yield up to the bow-bearing Mede."

The patriotic spirit displayed by these ladies would probably make Simonides somewhat indulgent to any defects in their private or public character.

As we are about to leave Simonides for the present, it may not be out of place here to comment upon the blame which has been attached to his conduct in connection with the family of Pisistratus. Notwithstanding the kindness that he had received from Hipparchus and his brother, and the friendship that subsisted between them and him, he allowed himself to celebrate the assassination of Hipparchus (for it deserves no other name), in a well-known epigram, which may be thus translated:—

"Truly a great light met the Athenians' view,
What time his sword Aristogiton drew,
And, with Harmodius' help, Hipparchus slew."

Blamable as this may appear, there may have been excuses for Simonides's conduct which are not fully manifest. He may have seen or thought that the Athenian genius required for its full development greater freedom than was afforded by an absolute Government; or he may have seen in the individual rulers faults of character which were dangerous to liberty. Hippias, after his brother's death, became a ruthless tyrant; and when he was himself displaced, his conduct in joining the Persians, and in instigating and assisting to organise their invasion of Attica, showed him to be destitute of true magnanimity, principle, or patriotism.

The feeling of the Athenians, as excited by the victories which they gained over the Persian invaders, and particularly their earliest triumph at Marathon, were of a striking character. They seem to have experienced little personal elation, and to have been strongly impressed with the danger of indulging in any self-laudation or assumption of personal merit. Pagans as they were, they had something of that humility which, under a nobler dispensation, inspired the psalm of "Non nobis, Domine." "The victory," as observed by Thirlwall, "was viewed by the people as a deliverance which could not have been effected by their own arm without the friendly interposition of a higher power." Hence their dedication to Nemesis. Hence their belief in the interposition of Pan, and their erection of a statue to him. "Hence the wonderful legends of the battle: the valiant Epizelus is blinded in the heat of the fight by the apparition of a warrior, whose shield is covered by his flowing beard: the local heroes are active in the combat; and in the picture that represented it on the walls of the Painted Porch, Theseus appeared rising out of the ground with Marathon and Hercules; and the hero Echetlus, armed with a ploughshare, was seen dealing death among the flying barbarians: hence to this day the field of Marathon is believed to be haunted, as in the time of Pausanias, with spectral warriors, and the shepherds are alarmed in the night by their shouts, and by the neighing of their steeds."

Simonides, who so nobly celebrated these noble exploits, was not himself a soldier; but Æschylus was a soldier as well as a poet. He fought at Marathon; and there seems to have been a tradition that he competed unsuccessfully with Simonides for an elegy on those who fell in battle on that field. He died at an advanced age at Gela, in Sicily, and is said to have written an epitaph on himself which the inhabitants of Gela inscribed on a monument erected in his honour. The epitaph, of which a translation is here subjoined, is remarkable for its making mention of his military achievements without adverting to his literary success:—

> "Athenian Æschylus, Euphorion's son,
> This tomb at Gela holds, his race now run.
> His deeds, the grove of Marathon could tell,
> And many a long-haired Median knows them well."

There also distinguished himself, at Marathon, a brother of Æschylus, Cynegirus, another son of Euphorion's. This man, who became an almost fabulous hero of Greece, clung with his hands to the side of a Persian vessel that was retreating, and, when one hand was cut off, held on by the other till that also was severed, when he fell dead. The fame of an action like this, as gallant at least as that of Witherington in the ballad of "Chevy Chase," lost nothing in the subsequent telling of it; and the tradition came to be that, after his second hand was cut off, he tried to stop the vessel with his teeth. The following epigram was at a later period composed upon a portrait of him by Phasis, which represented him with both his hands:—

> "Blest Cynegirus, some think Phasis wrong
> In giving you those hands, so stout and strong:
> No; he was wise those hands to let us see
> By which you gained your immortality."

Another of the pre-eminent heroes of Greece whose reputation for bravery has been elevated to a proverbial celebrity is the Spartan Othryades, who was one of three hundred of his countrymen selected to fight with an equal number of Argives for the sovereignty of Thyrea, a frontier town between Laconia and Argolis. The battle was bravely contested on both sides, till there remained only two of the Argives, who, believing themselves to be the sole survivors of the six hundred, returned to Argos to announce their victory. In fact, however, Othryades, the last of the Spartans, though struck down and bleeding, was still alive, and upon the departure of the Argives collected together the shields and weapons of the enemy, and erected or hung them up as a trophy, surmounted with his own shield, on which he wrote in his blood the words, "Thyrea, Jupiter, belongs to the Lacedemonians." Upon this ground, as proving that Othryades had kept the field when the Argives had either fallen or fled, the Spartans claimed the victory, and successfully maintained their right in a general battle.

Upon this event two epigrams are preserved, one written as from the Spartan, the other as from the Argive side of the question :—

> "When, native Sparta, the Inachian band
> We fought, in numbers matched, for Thyrea's land,
> Thy brave three hundred never turned aside,
> But where our feet were planted there we died.
> The words that on his shield Othryades,
> Claiming the victory, wrote with blood were these:
> 'Thyrea is Sparta's, Jove.' If it be said
> That any Argive from that combat fled,
> He owns Adrastus' kin: 'tis death to fly,
> So Sparta deems :—It is not death to die."

In the other epigram, as on the side of the Argives,

the two survivors are supposed to have returned to the field, where they find the expiring Spartan lying beside the trophy which he had set up, and which their religious scruples prevented them from destroying:—

> "Who hung those new-ta'en arms upon the tree?
> What on this Dorian targe may written be?
> The Thyrean ground with hostile blood is dyed,
> And we two of our friends alone abide.
> Seek out each fallen foe, that none may claim,
> Living, a false increase to Sparta's fame.
> But stay! in blood Othryades' red shield
> For Sparta claims the honours of the field,
> While he now gasps for breath. O righteous Jove!
> These signs of unjust victory reprove."

The traditional fame enjoyed by these two heroes, Cynegirus and Othryades, may be seen from a much later epigram (if an epigram it may be called) by Crinagoras upon the valour of an Italian soldier, though it may scarcely be thought that what this hero accomplished deserved the flourish of trumpets with which his story is introduced:—

> "Tell us not of Cynegirus,
>   Leave Othryades unsung;
> Other deeds to-day inspire us,
>   Claiming praise from every tongue.
> In the Rhine's well-watered region,
>   Where a Roman soldier lay,
> See! the eagle of his legion
>   Carried by the foe away!
> Though his strength and life were sinking,
>   Bravely he resolved to rise;

>   Faced the captor without shrinking,
>   And regained the precious prize.
>   When the standard, thus recovered,
>   To its ancient guards had passed,
>   Triumph o'er his features hovered,
>   And in joy he breathed his last."

It may be a relief to get out of these warlike themes to a calmer region, and to see the tendencies of the Greek mind, in those dedications to the divine powers which seem to have been habitually practised in private life. It will be interesting to follow these through the different stages at which they occurred.

Here is one which sets forth the prayer and offering of a young maiden, apparently with the concurrence of her mother; or perhaps it is the prayer of a mother for her daughter, addressed to Rhea, the mother of the gods, for a prosperous life,—not forgetting an eligible establishment in marriage. The author is Leonidas of Tarentum, a pleasing and voluminous epigrammatist, belonging apparently to the third century B.C. The translation is by Merivale:—

>   "O holy Mother! on the peak
>   Of Dindyma, and on those summits bleak
>   That frown on Phrygia's scorched plain,
>   Holding thy throne,—with fav'ring aspect deign
>   To smile on Aristodicè,
>   Seilenè's virgin child, that she
>   May grow in beauty and her charms improve
>   To fulness, and invite connubial love.
>   For this, thy porch she seeks, with tributes rare,
>   And o'er thine altars strews her votive hair."

The next, by an anonymous author, contains a minute account of the dedication to Diana by a virgin " about to marry" of her girlish playthings and head-dress :—

> " Timaretè, her wedding-day now near,
>   To Artemis has laid these offerings here,—
> Her tambourine, her pleasant ball, the net
>   As a safe guardian o'er her tresses set ;
> Her maiden dolls, in mimic robes arrayed,
>   Gifts fitting for a maid to give a maid.
> Goddess, thy hand upon her kindly lay,
>   And keep her holy in thy holy way."

The next is from a matron who dedicates her gifts and thanks to three goddesses for the multiplied boons with which her life has been enriched : it is by Agathias :—

> " To Venus garlands—braids of clustering hair
>   To Pallas, and her zone to Artemis,
> Callirrhoè gave—fit tributes offered there,
>   Whence to her lot had fallen a triple bliss.
> A loved and loving suitor she had wed,
>   In modest purity her life was led,
> And a male race of children blessed her bed."

A matron thus returns her thanks for the interesting event of the birth of twins. It is by Leonidas, and is addressed to the Goddess of Parturition :—

> " Here, Ilethyia, at thy noble feet
>   Ambrosia lays a grateful offering meet—
> A robe and head-dress—favoured by thy power
>   In the sore travail of her perilous hour;
> And in due season strengthened to bring forth
>   A double offspring at a happy birth."

A young lad here makes an offering to Mercury of the childish things which he was then laying aside. It is by Leonidas:—

"To Hermes, this fair ball of pleasant sound,
This boxen rattle, fraught with lively noise,
These maddening dice, this top well whirling round,—
Philocles has hung up, his boyhood's toys."

This is another, by Euphorion, recording the consecration by a young man of the first-fruits of his hair to Apollo, possibly at Delphi—a ceremony which was performed as a religious act—the hair at Athens and elsewhere in Greece being cut for the first time on the termination of boyhood. The youth referred to appears, from the allusion to ivy, to have shown poetical aspirations, of which an ivy wreath would be the appropriate reward:—

"When first Eudoxus cut the locks he wore,
That charm of boyhood he to Phœbus bore;
Instead of locks, Far-darter, hear his vow,
And let Acharnian ivy wreath his brow."

Our next epigram, by an uncertain author, shows the youth advancing towards manhood:—

"Lycon, the rising down that first appeared,
To Phœbus gave, the presage of a beard;
And prayed that so he might in after-years,
On his grey locks, as now, employ the shears.
Grant this request, and on his age bestow
The honour that should crown a head of snow."

Just as the youth made an offering of the things of

his childhood, and the incipient young man of the signs of his adolescence, so the worn-out labourer or craftsman devoted to some deity the implements which he could no longer wield. Thus, a fisherman offers his net, in an epigram by Julian the Egyptian. He has written several on the same subject, but we take the shortest as a specimen :—

> "Old Cyniras to the Nymphs this net: no more
> His strength can stand the toils that once it bore:
> Rejoice, ye fishes, sporting in the sea,
> From danger at his hands you now are free."

There was no want of offerings to the gods, particularly to those connected with husbandry, as an inducement to grant the votary's prayer for continued or increased abundance. Biton, an old man, makes offerings to three deities to propitiate their favour in protecting and increasing his rural wealth. The epigram we give is by Sabinus, and runs thus :—

> "Roses, the Nymphs,—and Pan, a kid—received in this green shade
> From Biton; and for Bacchus too a thyrsus here he laid.
> Accept the gifts, and prosper well, ye several Powers Divine,—
> Pan and the Nymphs, the flocks and founts,—Bacchus, the joyous wine."

We have just had an example of offerings by one person to three deities; we shall now give, from Leonidas, a record of offerings made to one deity by three comrades, employed in several forms of hunting or capture, but all of them, it would appear, carried on by means of the net. There are many editions of this idea by different authors, but we prefer that of Leonidas, which is the shortest of them :—

> "Three brothers dedicate, O Pan, to thee,
> Their nets, the various emblems of their toil;
> Pigres, who brings from realms of air his spoil,
> Dames, from woods, and Clitor from the sea.
> So may the treasures of the deep be given
> To this—to those the fruits of earth, and heaven."

Leaving the dry land, we give an epigram recording the offering to the sea-gods by a man saved from shipwreck. It is by Lucian :—

"To Glaucus, Nereus, Ino, and to Melicerte as well,
To Neptune, and the mystic powers in Samothrace that dwell,
Grateful that, from the sea preserved, he now on shore can live,
Lucillus cuts and gives these hairs—'tis all he has to give."

This is a similar tribute in an epigram by Diodorus :—

> "When, the wind stirring the Carpathian main,
> The yard gave way in that night's hurricane,
> Diogenes, beholding, made the vow
> That from impending fate if rescued now,
> Cabeirus, great Bœotian god, to thee
> He would, within thy precincts hang up ME—
> A little garment—this he now performs.
> Oh! save him both from poverty and storms."

In each of these last two epigrams allusion is made to the Cabiri, who, being worshipped originally in Egypt, became Samothracian divinities, and were worshipped also in Bœotia. It was believed that those who were initiated in their mysteries would be saved in a storm at sea upon appealing to them for preservation.

Here is a dedication of the offerer's ship itself, which is no longer to go to sea, and along with which he has bid farewell to a seafaring life and its vicissitudes. It is by Macedonius :—

> "King of the sea, and Ruler of the shore,
> This ship, ordained to touch the waves no more,
> I, Crantas, give to thee,—a ship long driven
> In sport before the wandering winds of heaven ;
> In which, oft sailing, I have thought with dread,
> I soon might reach the regions of the dead.
> Renouncing winds and waves, and hope and fear,
> Now on dry land I fix my footstep here."

The conceptions of the Greeks in their votive offerings were often of a fanciful kind. The epigram that follows, said to be by Plato (but probably not the philosopher), proceeds upon this incident, real or supposed :
"A traveller who, when nearly exhausted by thirst, is guided by the croaking of a frog to a spring of water, dedicates to the Nymphs a bronze image of his preserver."

The following translation, though not so ambitious as some we have before us, is nearer the original :—

> " The servant of the Nymphs, who loves the showers,
> The minstrel moist, who lurks in watery bowers,
> A frog, in bronze, a Wayfarer here laid,
> Whose burning thirst was quenched by welcome aid.
> By the hoarse monitor's amphibious tone
> A hidden spring was to the wanderer shown.
> He followed, nor forsook the guiding sound
> Till the much-wished-for draught he grateful found."

In a remarkable epigram by Leonidas, Mars is made to reject with indignation the dedication to himself of arms that had never seen military service. The translation is Mr Hodgson's:—

> "Away with spoils like these!—they are not mine;—
> Hateful to Mars, nor worthy of his shrine:
> Uncleft the helm, unstained with blood the shield,
> The inglorious spear, unbroken in the field.
> Reddening with shame, I feel the hot drops flow,
> In scorn for cowards, from my blushing brow.
> These, let some lover range in wanton pride
> Round nuptial halls and chambers of the bride.
> Hung in the temple of the god of fight
> Arms dropping gore; for such his soul delight."

The next epigram we shall give records an interesting dedication of a quiver and arrows by a father who, by a feat of archery somewhat similar to that of William Tell, had saved his little son's life, and was resolved that weapons once used for so beneficent a purpose should never more be employed in the work of destruction:—

> "Alcon beheld his boy, while laid to rest,
> Close in a deadly serpent's folds compressed:
> He bent his bow with hand that thrilled with dread,
> But did not miss his mark—the arrow sped
> Right thro' the monster's jaws with prosperous aim,
> Near, but not touching, the dear infant's frame.
> His quiver, fraught with shafts devised to kill,
> Hangs on this oak, released from working ill,
> A record of good fortune and good skill."

The story on which Gætulicus, its author, has founded this inscription, is referred to by several ancient writers as well known. The boy thus saved is said to have been named Phalerus, and subsequently to have become one of the Argonauts.

Another of the dedicatory class of epigrams to which we shall refer is one of the most celebrated of all, and is ascribed to one of the greatest names among the anthological poets. It is the dedication by Lais to Venus of her looking-glass, of which the author is said to be Plato the philosopher. It has been imitated by Prior in the well-known quatrain:—

> "Venus! take this votive glass,
> Since I am not what I was:
> What I shall hereafter be,
> Venus! let me never see."

Neat as these lines are, and involving the essential ideas of the epigram, they are not sufficiently full or so like the original as might be wished. We give what follows, out of many literal versions which have been attempted:—

> "Lais, who smiled at Greece with scornful pride,
> I, at whose doors a swarm of lovers sighed,
> This glass to Venus: since what I shall be
> I would not, what I was, I cannot, see."

Plato's epigram was imitated and expanded by Julian the Egyptian, of which the following, though rather a condensed version, will show the additional points that Julian introduced:—

> "I, Lais, who on conquered Greece looked down with
>   haughty pride;
> I, to whose courts in other days a swarm of lovers hied,

O, ever lovely Venus! now this mirror give to thee;
For my present self I would not, and my past I cannot
    see."

The general idea of a beautiful woman relinquishing her looking-glass on discovering that her charms begin to wane, presents a picture that has in it both a shade of sadness and a touch of satire. Apart from its mechanical uses, her looking-glass, it must be confessed, is no unimportant element in a woman's life; and it may be said to be a necessary help to her attaining that complete self-knowledge at which all should aim. It is right that a woman should know whether she is beautiful or not. Socrates is said to have enjoined all young persons to look often into their glass to ascertain if they were good-looking—that, if they were so, they might strive to make their mental attainments correspond; and if they were not so, then that they might endeavour by the superior accomplishments of their minds to compensate for their personal shortcomings. The fondness for this species of self-contemplation seems to be strong in the sex in general. Novelists describe the village coquette as delighting to admire her face in a small fragment of a looking-glass; and in one of Southey's books we are told of the poor Portuguese nuns who had never seen the reflection of themselves from the time of entering their place of seclusion until the nunneries were thrown open by the effects of the French invasion. The first impulse of them all was to fly to a looking-glass that they might see their own faces—a sight which to most of them would seem strange indeed, and would inflict the same kind of pain that Lais was determined to avoid. Ovid somewhere tells a lady—

"The time will come when this your old delight,
Your mirror, will present no pleasant sight."

This era, at which a woman's looking-glass becomes distasteful to her, must bring with it a severe trial and a crisis in her character. In a light French comedy a handsome and gay widow is one day found by her friends and admirers to be in a very wayward mood, the explanation of which, on careful inquiry, is found to be that she had that morning observed in her glass the first wrinkle that had visited her face. It must require in the case of an established beauty no small degree of good-humour, good sense, and strength of mind to submit cheerfully to the change thus commencing; and it will be well for her if she has already followed the advice that Ovid gives to a young woman :—

"Build up the Mind to prop frail Beauty's power!
The mind alone lasts to life's latest hour." *

But Plato's epigram will not let us confine our attention to the general aspect of the situation; we are compelled to look at it with special reference to Greek manners, and in particular to that painful subject, the condition of women in Greece. Whatever liberty women may have enjoyed in the heroic or earlier times,

---

* The beauty who thus passes into the list of Has-been's may, however, console herself with the sentiment expressed by a clever wit to a plain-looking woman who was taunting by that epithet a veteran belle, that "the *Has-been's* were at least better than the *Never-was-es*."

it is certain that in Greek society in its more advanced period, and especially at Athens in the time of Plato, the position of the Greek wife presented a strange contrast to that of the foreign companion. The wife was certainly not the companion of her husband. She was the mother and the nurse of his children, and the housekeeper or upper servant in his establishment; and though she partook of his meals when they were alone, she rarely did so when other men were present, and never joined in his feasts or convivial meetings. Her place was in the seclusion of home, from which she only emerged, if at all, under rigid restrictions. In a degree corresponding with these servile duties and restraints seems to have been the cultivation or want of cultivation of the women's minds, which rendered them little capable of holding any enlightened intercourse with their husbands or sympathising in any intellectual pursuits. As to education, young women may be said to have had none; and their time must indeed have been drearily passed. We may here quote an epigram of Agathias on the subject, who lived at a much later period, when a glimpse of better things must have been introduced from the growing influence of Christian feelings. It is in the form of a complaint put into the mouth of a susceptible Greek maiden, and shows that even in that day the old habits had not yet disappeared. The version is by Mr Swayne:—

> "Ah! youths never know the weight of care,
> That delicate-spirited women must bear.
> For comrades of cheery speech have they,
> To blandish the woes of thought away:

With games they can cheat the hours at home,
And whenever abroad in the streets they roam
With the colours of painting they glad themselves.
But as for us, poor prisoned elves,
We are shut out from sunlight, buried in rooms,
And fretted away by our fancy's glooms."

In strong contrast with the position of the Greek maiden and matron of respectable and native parentage was that of the foreign women who were found in Greece. On turning to Mr Theodore Martin's volume on Horace in this series, p. 109, the reader will find an account of the *demi-monde* that frequented Rome; but still more conspicuous and attractive were the Greek Hetairæ, whose headquarters may be said to have been Corinth. Just as the native Greek women were excluded from society, these foreigners—whose number seems to have been swelled by the addition sometimes of foundlings, who had no recognised parentage—were excluded from marriage; no union that they could form being other than temporary or precarious in law. Aspasia was as much the wife of Pericles as the law would allow; but when he lost the two legitimate sons that his first and lawful wife brought him, he could not look to his boy by Aspasia as in any respect entitled to the status of a son; and it was only by an act of special grace that the young man was legitimised by the Athenian people, and added to his father's tribe with his father's name.

In this degraded position these "strange" women were brought up, with all the accomplishments of which the female mind is capable, and with all the arts of allurement that could attract and fix their lovers, so far at least as such accomplishments and attractions can be attained without the support of moral dignity. Singing and instrumental music, dancing and sprightly conversation, were their special subjects of study; and some of them, such as Aspasia, seem also to have been educated in the highest and most intellectual acquirements. Supposing it to have been a satirical or exaggerated statement that Aspasia composed the best of Pericles's speeches, the suggestion would have had no point unless she was believed to have possessed a high degree of genius and cultivation. It was these women who were the "companions" of men, and specially of young men, in their convivial repasts, when women were admitted at all; and it was their powers of amusement and hilarity that constituted their most delightful and most dangerous charm. This was a miserable state of society, in which an impassable gulf intervened between the Virtuous and the Attractive; and a serious reflection must here awaken our minds to a strong sense of the social benefits which, besides other blessings, Christianity has conferred on us, in elevating the position of women as compared with the place they have occupied under other systems of religion, whether Pagan or Mohammedan.

The epigrams just quoted as to Lais have a plain reference to her condition as an alien. Her birthplace seems to be unknown; but if it was Corinth, she cannot have inherited the right of citizenship. She is represented as looking with scorn on Greece as a country which she had conquered and laid captive at her feet; but it is easy to see with what bitterness and deep melancholy a woman with her history and her prospects must have regarded the impending loss of that beauty which, however aided by mental qualities and acquirements, must have been the chief basis of her great but precarious and transitory influence. We shall dismiss this imperial and imperious beauty by giving an epigram by Antipater of Sidon, upon her general character and situation, though it belongs properly to the class of epitaphs, and comes in here only as an illustration of what has above been said. The translation is by Hay:—

> "Lais, who walked in gold and purple dyes,
> Here on her sea-girt Corinth lowly lies—
> The pampered friend of Eros, whom that elf
> Nurtured more daintily than Venus' self.
> Brighter this human goddess than the stream,
> Which in Pirenè sheds its fulgent gleam:
> And wooers more she had who sought her arms,
> Than ever sighed for brilliant Helen's charms.
> And many revelled in those graces—sold
> For the false glare of all subduing gold.
> Even in her ashes lives the rich perfume
> Of odours ever floating round her tomb:
> Steeped are her locks in myrrh; the buxom air
> Inhales the fragrance of her essenced hair.
> And when she died, Cythera near her stood
> With grief-soiled cheeks, and Eros sobbed aloud.
> Oh! if these charms so many had not bought,
> Greece had for Lais as for Helen fought."

Let us add here, that whatever may have been the general tendency of Greek manners in these respects, there could never be wanting cases in which nature would assert her rights, and a pure affection be formed between young lovers, terminating in wedlock. We shall hereafter see some proofs of the truth of this remark.

It was, we have seen, a prominent part of the Greek and Roman religions to deify, or connect with deity, the most attractive or most important natural objects —particularly rivers, fountains, and trees. These seem often to have been regarded as themselves divine; but at least they were held to be inhabited or frequented by divine beings, or were placed under their protection. Fountains, so invaluable a boon in a warm climate, are special favourites. Horace, in one of the most delightful of his odes, which our readers will find in the appropriate volume of this series, at p. 72, vows to sacrifice a kid to the fountain of Bandusia in return for the cool refreshment it afforded. At this present time Celtic antiquaries in France are busied in tracing the signs of Water-worship in pagan ages, and think, perhaps fancifully, that in various names of rivers, such as the Dee, the Don, the Devon, there is an affinity with the ancient terms for Deity or Divinity—an etymology which seems long ago to have occurred to the Latin poet Ausonius, who was a Frenchman by birth. This is a translation of one of his lines referring to the chief city of the tribe of the Cadurci, where there was a great aqueduct:—

" The Celtic Divŏna, a fount divine."

Some epigrams on the subject of fountains or streams

have already been given. Here is another by Hermocreon:—

> "Ye water-nymphs, to whom Hermocreon placed
> These gifts, when a fresh fountain here he found,
> Hail! and when those fair feet my home have graced,
> Be filled with the pure streams that flow around."

The epigram that follows is, as will be seen, an imaginary dedication, as it relates to an historical or rather a legendary character, Neoptolemus, or Pyrrhus as he was called from the fiery colour of his hair, the son of Achilles and descendant of Æacus, monarch of Ægina. The epigram seems to represent Neoptolemus, whose entry into public life was very warlike, as now settling down to rural employments, and making simple offerings to the divinities by whom he was surrounded:—

> "Ye folds, ye hill-nymphs' haunts, ye fountains clear
> Under the cliff, thou pine-tree rising near,
> Thou square-formed Hermes, saviour of the flock,
> And Pan, thou dweller on the goat-browsed rock,
> See here the gifts I bring, in hope to please,—
> Cakes and a wine-cup full—accept of these
> From Neoptolemus Æacides."

The only reference in this epigram which seems to need explanation is the allusion to Hermes or Mercury, who is spoken of as the "square-formed." This was the general shape of those Hermæ, the images which were so frequent as measurements of distances or marks of boundaries, consisting of a rude square figure with a head but no hands. More recondite explanations of the epithet are sometimes given, as that the dexterity of the god in all situations was such, that like a cube he always alighted upon a stable basis ; or that he was the inventor of the four great discoveries of letters, music, gymnastics, and geometry. Mention is made by Pausanias of a square figure of Mercury made of stone, placed beside images of the Nymphs, and with a stream of water issuing from his left hand.

Here is an offering to some aquatic deities from a thirsty traveller—by Leonidas of Tarentum :—

"Cool stream, where waters from the cleft rock start,
Forms, too, of Naiads, carved by rustic art,
Ye fountain-heads, and countless spots around,
Made lovely by your rills that here abound,
Farewell ! and from a wayfarer receive,
The horn which here he dipped his hot thirst to relieve."

It is from the statues or images thus placed near fountains or in beautiful spots of scenery that we may suppose the invitations to proceed, which the epigrams so often address to us, to seek rest or refreshment. Here are some specimens. This is anonymous, supposed to be spoken by Pan from his image near a fountain :—

"Come, rest beneath my pine-tree, murmuring sweet
  To the soft zephyrs it delights to greet :
  Here, by this limpid stream that gurgling flows,
  My rustic pipe shall soothe you to repose."

This by Anytê is very similar; the translation altered from Bland :—

"Stranger, beneath this rock thy limbs bestow,
    Sweet in the green leaves the breeze murmurs here:
This fountain's stream will cool the summer's glow:
    Such rest is ever to tired pilgrims dear."

This is by Hermocreon, also very like:—

"Sit, passer-by, this plane-tree's shade beneath,
Whose leaves are stirred when soft the zephyrs breathe:
Here I am stationed, Maia's son renowned,
To guard Nicagoras' goods and fruitful ground."

This, again, is by Anytè:—

"To shaggy Pan, and to the Fold-nymphs fair,
    Fast by the rock a shepherd's offering stands,
Theudotus' gift to those who gave him there
Rest, when he fainted in the sultry air,
    And reached him sweetest water with their hands."

This is by Myro of Byzantium, the translation by Mr Burgon:—

"O forest-nymphs! O daughters of the river,
Who haunt ambrosial these deep glades for ever
    With rosy feet,
Thrice hail! and be Cleonymus your care:
For he, in this pine-sheltered, calm retreat,
To you erected all these statues fair."

This chapter may be appropriately closed by two little poems of a character closely resembling each other, as referring to places, perhaps towers or small temples in the sea or on the seaside, dedicated to Venus, in her pleasing character as Queen of the Sea, and as protecting sailors by the soothing or subduing influence of her image on the surrounding waves.

The first of these is by Anyte :—

> "This Venus' favourite haunt: 'tis her delight
> To look from land upon the ocean bright,
> And speed the sailor's course. The ambient brine
> Quails as it sees the image in her shrine."

Of the other, by Antipater, we shall give a translation by Mr Hay ; but in which a slight alteration has been made, for a reason that will be explained. It is Venus that speaks :—

> "Simple this shrine, where by the dark white wave
> I sit, the mistress of a briny shore :
> Simple, but loved ; for I delight to save
> The sailor, *while I quell the billows' roar.*
> Propitiate Venus : I will prove to thee
> A friend, when tossed by love or on the clear blue sea."

Lessing conjectures that the abode thus described may have been some seaside chapel to the marine Venus, such as may have been in use at Sestos, where Hero— Leander's Hero—officiated as a priestess of the goddess. He suggests that at such a chapel an image of Venus may have been preserved, which was lifted up or exposed to view in a storm in order to awe the waves into a state of calm. The idea in the epigram, therefore, seems to be, that Venus delights, not, as had been supposed, in the roaring of the billows, but in exerting her power to make them cease to roar.

On the gems and coins of Sestos or Abydos which refer to the story of Hero and Leander, a tower was sometimes to be seen, with Hero holding out a torch to guide her lover on his way.

CHAPTER III.

SEPULCHRAL.

We proceed now to that class of inscriptions which may be called Sepulchral, and which are of universal use among nations. Wordsworth, in his "Essay on Epitaphs," is anxious to prove the proposition of Weever in his 'Funeral Monuments,' that the invention of such inscriptions proceeded from the presage or anticipation of immortality implanted in all men naturally. He himself says, that "without the consciousness of immortality in the human soul, man could never have had awakened in him the desire to live in the remembrance of his fellows; mere love, or the yearning of kind towards kind, could not have produced it." There is much to support the views which Wordsworth urges on this subject. Many national customs have been manifestly formed on this basis; and it cannot be doubted that without the conviction that our nature possesses an imperishable part, our dispositions, affections, and aspirations would be lamentably changed for the worse, and the best light of our existence extinguished. But it does not seem to be certain either that a desire of posthumous reputation could not exist, or that a regard and respect for the memory and remains of those we loved when in life, could not be cherished and expressed, without the presage of immortality. Even those heathens, if such there be, who are without such a blessed anticipation, may yet look back with tender regret on the vanished happiness which they enjoyed with a beloved object; and the feeling of reverence which was directed to the living friend or parent may naturally extend to the lifeless body that was recently so dear to us. The sentiment, "how much less precious it is to associate with survivors than to remember the departed," does not seem to be indissolubly connected with any creed as to a future life; and the desire to defend from injury the bodies of friends is intelligible on other principles. Gray, in his "Elegy," ascribes the use of monumental erections and their inscriptions to a lower range of feeling:—

" Yet even these bones *from insult to protect*,
 Some frail memorial still erected nigh,
With uncouth rhymes and shapeless sculpture decked,
 Implores the passing tribute of a sigh."

It is perhaps a fault in the "Elegy in a Country Churchyard"—if it is permissible to find any fault in that admirable poem—that it should throughout exhibit so little of an appeal to religious feelings, or a direct reference to the prospect of immortality. But it may tend to show that a solemn and powerful regard for the dead has in some degree an independent basis. It has been a subject of grave doubt to some minds whether the earlier Jews were believers in a future state, and were not rather under the awe of a present theocracy; and the Book of Psalms has been referred to as at once the most religious of manuals, and yet the one which has the least clear indications of a life to come. It seems quite intelligible that the memory of parents and other ancestors, who have been benefactors to their kind, may be cherished, and memorials erected to them, not only from intrinsic regard and admiration, but also from a desire to stimulate their successors to imitate their virtues and equal their glory. The strong desire for posthumous fame shown by the ancient poets seems not wholly, and perhaps very partially, to arise from a religious feeling.

Greek epitaphs have a great diversity of character in this respect. Some of them make no allusion to a future state; and the absence of this hope seems only to make the feeling of bereavement more deep, and the recollection of what is lost more tender. Even these are, as Christopher North has said, "beautiful exceedingly; and in us, to whom life and immortality have been brought to light, they inspire a strange feeling of sympathy for such sadness, and of humble gratitude for our better lot. Heart-broken, hopeless sighs over the grave from which there might be no blessed resurrection! A lament as of the passing wind over the monumental stone! No bright gleam from above, as with us, cheering the gloom below! On the tombstone of the Christian maiden no words are graved utterly forlorn—much grief but no despair—being dead she yet speaketh—and the inscription is as a blessing on the survivors, who are bade weep no more for the happy."

We subjoin a few of the Greek epitaphs, beginning with two ascribed to Erinna, who is said, though without conclusive evidence, to have been a contemporary of Sappho. They are both upon a maiden friend of Erinna's, whose name was Baucis; but this appellation having unfortunately been appropriated by a respectable female of another character, our translators have substituted respectively Myrtis and Ida. This translation is by Elton :—

I.

"The virgin Myrtis' sepulchre am I:
 Creep softly to the pillared mount of woe,
 And whisper to the grave, in earth below,
 'Grave! thou art envious in thy cruelty!'
 To thee now gazing here, her barbarous fate
 These bride's adornments tell ;—that with the fire
 Of Hymen's torch which led her to the gate,
 Her husband burned the maid upon her pyre.
 Yes, Hymen! thou didst change the marriage-song
 To the shrill wailing of the mourners' throng."

Merivale has another version, of which the last part is so good as to deserve being also inserted :—

"The very torch that laughing Hymen bore
 To light the virgin to the bridegroom's door,
  With that same torch the bridegroom lights the fire
  That dimly glimmers on her funeral pyre.
 Thou, too, O Hymen! bid'st the nuptial lay
 In elegiac moanings die away."

II.

"Pillars of death! carved syrens! tearful urn!
  In whose sad keeping my poor dust is laid,
To those who near my tomb their footsteps turn,
  Stranger or Greek, bid hail! and say, a maid
Rests in her bloom below; her sire the name
  Of Myrtis gave; her birth and lineage high:
And say her bosom-friend Erinna came,
  And on this marble graved her elegy."

Here is a similar one by Meleager himself, translated by Wrangham :—

"Her virgin zone unloosed, Cleæra's charms
Death clasps—stern bridegroom—in his iron arms.
Hymns at the bridal valves last night were sung—
Last night the bridal roof with revels rung—
This morn the wail was raised, and, hushed and low,
The strains of joy were changed to moans of woe;
And the bright torch to Hymen's hall which led,
With mournful glare now lighted to the dead."

The following is said to be by Sappho. The translation is by Elton, a little altered :—

"This dust was Timas': ere her bridal bed
Within Persephone's dark bower received,
With new-sharped steel her playmates from each head
Cut their fair locks, to show how much they grieved."

This also is said to be Sappho's, translated by Charles Merivale :—

"Deep in the dreary chambers of the dead,
  Asteria's ghost has made her bridal bed.
Still to this stone her fond compeers may turn,
  And shed their cherished tresses on her urn."

But notwithstanding this prevailing gloom, there are, as Mr Merivale has said, "a few which present us with brighter prospects, and bring us nearer to the Elysium described by the more cheerful poets of Italy." One of the most gladsome of these is an epitaph upon "Proté," a name which means First, and indicates probably a first-born daughter. It is not in the regular Anthologies, but is a Greek inscription on a marble at Rome belonging to a Roman family of Pagan times. We give a version by Hay, altering merely one line and a word to come nearer to the original:—

> "Proté, thou art not dead ; but thou hast passed
> To better lands, where pleasures ever last—
> To bound in joy amidst the fairest flowers
> Of the blest isles, Elysium's blooming bowers.
> Thee nor the summer's heat nor winter's chill
> Shall e'er annoy—exempt from every ill:
> Nor sickness, hunger, thirst again distress ;
> Nor dost thou long for earthly happiness.
> Contented thou, remote from human woes,
> In the pure light which from Olympus flows."

In seeking to illustrate these diversified aspects of the Greek sepulchral inscriptions in reference to the presence or absence of the hope of a future life, we have passed over some of the very simplest of these epitaphs, which deserve attention. It may be interesting to follow them through the different periods of life, though a good many specimens of epitaphs on young women have already been given.

The following epitaph by Callimachus (B.C. 250) is an example of the severe simplicity and directness which the Greeks here aimed at. Everything essential is contained in it—the names of the persons, their mutual relations, the age of the buried boy, and the great hopes which he had held out to his father. There is no expression of grief, no effort at ornament, no expansion of any idea such as modern taste would suggest to a poet; the situation speaks for itself, and the very reticence of the bereaved parent gives to his sorrow a more solemn and sacred aspect.

The two versions we give are nearly literal:—

"His son, now twelve years old, Philippus sees
Here laid, his mighty hope, Nicoteles."

"His little son of twelve years old Philippus here has laid,
Nicoteles, on whom so much his father's hopes were stayed."

Here is another epitaph by Lucian on a still younger child, where the parents do not appear, and the child speaks somewhat philosophically in its own person:—

"A boy of five years old, serene and gay,
Unpitying Hades hurried me away.
Yet weep not for Callimachus; if few
The days I lived, few were my sorrows too."

We next give an epitaph on a young maiden, cut off in the prime of youth and beauty, while the "cynosure of neighbouring eyes." It is the composition of Anytè, a Tegean poetess, belonging apparently to the third century before our era, whose epigrams, twenty-two in number, possess great delicacy and tenderness of style, and procured for her the emblem of the "white lily," assigned to her by Meleager:—

"I mourn the maid Antibia, for whose love
　　Full many a suitor sought her father's hall,—
　Her beauty and her wit so much could move;
　　But deadly Fate o'erturned the hopes of all."

Here is another version by Mr Keen:—

' Drop o'er Antibia's grave a pious tear,
　For virtue, beauty, wit, lie buried here.
　Full many a suitor sought her father's hall,
　To gain the virgin's love; but death o'er all
　Claimed dire precedence—who shall death withstand?—
　Their hopes were blasted by his ruthless hand."

This is sweet and elegant, but not sufficiently simple or short. We add one by Mr Hay, which Christopher North declared that he considered perfect:—

"The maid Antibia I lament; for whom
　　Full many a suitor sought her father's hall:
　For beauty, prudence, famed was she; but doom
　　Destructive overwhelmed the hopes of all."

We now give another epitaph by Callimachus, simple and short, as his compositions generally are, but containing a lofty thought, always a favourite among the ancients as among ourselves:—

"Here Dicon's son, Acanthian Saon lies
　In sacred sleep: say not a good man *dies*."

The same idea, almost identically expressed, is contained in another, and apparently a later epitaph, by an unknown author:—

"This is Popilia's tomb: my husband's care
　Framed it,—Oceanus, of wisdom rare.
　Here rest my ashes; but the Shades below
　Hearing my hymns, thy goodness, friend, shall know.

Think of me ever, husband, and while here
Drop, on the tomb I fill, the frequent tear.
And say, Popilia slumbers : never think
That the good die: to happy sleep they sink."

It is a natural and precious belief, as to all the departed whom we value,—

" How *sleep* the Brave, who sink to rest
By all their country's wishes blest!"

Callimachus led us into this train of thought, and we shall follow it up by another epitaph of his upon a friend, written in his best style, much admired and often translated. As it is a model of its kind, we shall give three translations,—the first by a distinguished and lamented scholar, Henry Nelson Coleridge; the second by Mr Hay; and a third which we add with diffidence, as bringing out one or two points in the original which in the others seem a little lost sight of :—

" They told me, Heraclitus, thou wert dead,
And then I thought, and tears thereon did shed,
How oft we two talked down the sun ; but thou
Halicarnassean guest ! art ashes now.
Yet live thy nightingales of song : on those
Forgetfulness her hand shall ne'er impose."

" I wept, my Heraclitus, when they told
That thou wert dead ; I thought of days of old,—
How oft in talk we sent the sun to rest :
Long since hast thou, my Halicarnassian guest,
Been dust : yet live thy nightingales—on these
The all-plundering hand of death shall never seize."

"One told me, Heraclitus, of thy fate,
  Which brought the tear into my eye to think
How oft we two, conversing long and late,
  Have seen the sun into his chamber sink;
But that is past and gone, and somewhere thou,
  Halicarnassian guest! art ashes now.
Yet live those nightingales of thine; on these
  The all-grasping hand of Hades will not seize."

Here is another epitaph by a friend upon a friend, by an unknown author, but simple and beautiful as Callimachus himself might have written:—

"A record, good Sabinus, though unfit,
  This little stone of our great love shall be:
I still shall miss thee: thou, if law permit,
  Abstain from Lethe's wave for love of me."

The concluding idea in these lines has been copied in an epitaph in the Latin Anthology on a predeceasing wife, who is thus addressed by her husband:—

"But thou of touching Lethe's stream beware,
  Certain that soon thy husband will be there."

Friendship, so touchingly illustrated by the epitaphs immediately above quoted, seems, we think, to have played a more important or more conspicuous part in Greek manners and social history than it does among ourselves. It was necessarily so, indeed, considering the different character of domestic life in the two forms of national habits. It has sometimes been said that in our own country and age a man's best friend is generally to be found in his wife; and the identity of their interests, the equality of their position, and the correspondence between their attainments and intelligence, greatly conduce to this result, which is at the same time promoted by the very differences that exist in their tastes and faculties, and that give a peculiar softness and tenderness to their attachment.

Friendship, with us, is more peculiarly the virtue of youth; and no greater blessing can befall a young man than the friendship of one not much exceeding his own years, and from whom he may derive living lessons in the pursuit of learning and the practice of high principle. The influence of such a friend is all the more powerful because it is more persuasive and less dictatorial than the teaching of a guardian or other preceptor of more advanced age and of less congenial feelings.

The delightful glimpse that the epitaph on Heraclitus gives us of two friends conversing till they talked the sun down, reminds one of a still nobler picture in Cowley's admirable "Elegy on the Death of William Hervey:"—

> "Say, for you saw us, ye immortal lights,
> How oft unweary'd have we spent the nights,
> Till the Ledæan stars, so famed for love,
> Wondered at us from above?
> We spent them not in toys, or lust, or wine,
> But search of deep philosophy,
> Wit, eloquence, and poetry,
> Arts which I loved, for they, my friend, were thine."

We think we do our readers a great service by referring them here, if they do not already know it, to a very pleasing poem by Principal Shairp in 'Macmillan's Magazine' for March 1873, containing his touching reminiscences of the band of distinguished friends among whom his college days at Oxford had been passed.

We proceed to give some miscellaneous epitaphs on persons of both sexes dying in early life, or at least before old age.

This, by Hegesippus, is on a good man, and is interesting as referring to the two diverging roads in the Unseen Regions, mentioned also by Virgil, of which the one on the right leads to Elysium, and the other to Tartarus :—

"Hermes leads good men from the pyre, they say,
 To Rhadamanthus, by the right-hand way;
 Which Aristonöus, not unwept, has trod
 To all-compelling Pluto's wide abode."

This is on a young maiden named Macedonia, cut off before her prime, but described as having a marked superiority of character. It is by Paul the Silentiary :—

"Thy bier, and not thy bridal bed, sweet maid,
 With grieving hands thy parents have arrayed.
 Thou from life's troubles and from childbirth's pains
 Escap'st ; for them a cloud of woes remains.
 Fate, at thy twelfth year, wrapped thee in the mould—
 In beauty, young ; in moral merits, old."

Our next bears the name of Xenocritus, and laments the death at sea of a maiden who was repairing under her father's charge to her betrothed. The translation is partly borrowed from one by Mr Hay :—

"Shipwrecked Lysidicè, thou hapless fair,
  Lost in the sea, the brine bedews thy hair.
Ocean was stirred; and viewing the wild tide,
  Thou fell'st, in terror, from the vessel's side.
Thine and thy native Cuma's name are read
  On this void tomb, to tell that thou art dead.
Thy bones are somewhere washed in the cold deep;
  And Aristomachus, thy sire, must weep
That, journeying with thee for thy marriage-day,
  Nor bride, nor even her corse, he could convey."

We are afraid that the subject of the following lines had not possessed the "moral merits" ascribed to one young person already mentioned. It seems pretty clear from her companionable qualities that Patrophilè was not a Greek citizen; but her early death might be sad enough for all that, and a deep affliction to some one. The translation is based on one by Mr Hay:—

"In the full ripeness of thy beauty's prime,
  Thine eyelids now, Patrophilè, are sealed:
Mute is that tongue that so beguiled the time;
  Quenched are the wiles thy words and looks revealed.
The voice of harp and song—where, where are these?
  The kisses, too, that blest the circling bowl?
Why, Pluto, thus our loved companion seize?
  Had Venus maddened even thy gloomy soul?"

Commentators are not agreed as to the relation in which Meleager stood to some of the females to whom his verses were addressed, and in particular to Heliodora, who is the subject of one of the most beautiful and passionate laments that affection has ever prompted. We will believe that she was his wife, though some think she was his mistress, and high authorities infer from certain expressions used that she was his daughter. It has often been translated. The version we give is the joint production of Mr Hay and Christopher North. Several others of much merit will be found collected in 'Blackwood,' vol. xxxiv. p. 127; but it is sufficient to refer to them.

"Tears, Heliodora! tears for thee, companion of the dead,
Last yearnings of thy husband's love, to Hades now I shed;
Tears from a heart by anguish wrung for her whom I deplore—
Memorials of regretful love upon her tomb I pour.
For thee, belov'd, even with the dead, thy Meleager sighs,
Now parting with a precious gift which Acheron will not prize.
Where my desirèd blossom now? its bloom hath Hades spoiled,
And my consummate flower, alas! the cruel dust hath soiled.
Thou all-sustaining Mother, Earth! oh, clasp her to thy breast,
My evermore lamented one,—and softly let her rest!"

This next epitaph has a dramatic character about it which deserves notice. It is by Leonidas of Tarentum:—

"Who, and whose child art thou, who here dost lie
Under this marble?" "Prexo named am I,
The daughter of Calliteles." "Where born?"
"In Samos." "O'er thy tomb, say, who did mourn?"
"Theocritus, the spouse my parents chose."
"What caused thy death?" "Childbirth my days did close."
"How old?" "Just twenty-two." "No child didst leave?"
"Calliteles but three years old must grieve."

"Blessings and length of days be on the boy."
"Thanks, friend, and fortune's smiles mayst thou enjoy."

Here is another dialogue by Julian in a different style, the translation by Goldwin Smith :—

"Cruel is Death." "Nay, kind. He that is ta'en
  Was old in wisdom, though his years were few."
"Life's pleasure hath he lost." "Escaped life's pain :"
  "Nor wedded joys,"—"nor wedded sorrows, knew."

Here is a sweet epitaph by a husband who has sustained the double loss of a wife and child, by Bianor, the translation also by Goldwin Smith, slightly altered :—

"I wept Theonoë's loss ; but one fair child
Its father's heart of half its woe beguiled :
And now, sole source of hope and solace left,
That one fair child the envious Fates have reft.
Hear, Proserpine, my prayer, and lay to rest
My little babe on its lost mother's breast."

Take some specimens now relating to men older in years, who had run their career and accomplished their objects in life. This one is anonymous, the translation by Hodgson and Bland. It gives a pleasant picture of a useful country gentleman :—

"Take old Amyntor to thy heart, dear soil,
In kind remembrance of his former toil ;
Who first enriched and ornamented thee
With many a lovely shrub and branching tree,
And lured a stream to fall in artful showers
Upon thy thirsting herbs and fainting flowers.
First in the spring he knew the rose to rear ;
First in the autumn culled the ripened pear ;

His vines were envied all the country round,
And favouring heaven showered plenty on his ground;
Therefore, kind Earth, reward him in thy breast
With a green covering and an easy rest."

We shall now insert some examples of epitaphs on fishermen and mariners, who formed so numerous a class in the essentially maritime country of Greece. This is ascribed to Sappho :—

" Here, where the fisher Pelagon is laid,
His sire Meniscos has this offering made :
A wicker net and oar, that well may show
The life that fishers lead of toil and woe."

Sappho's epigram is only a couplet, and it is not easy to imitate the simplicity and condensation of the original; but this is an attempt :—

" Here to the fisher Pelagon, his sire Meniscos laid
A wicker-net and oar, to show his weary life and trade."

The next is by Addœus, on a fisherman whose boat was put to three various uses :—

" The fisher Diotimus long a trusty boat had rowed,
Which also furnished on dry land a poor but fit abode.
When thrown into his last long sleep, his dreary way he made
To Hades without further help, by that same boat conveyed :
For that which had sustained his life the old man kept entire,
And dying found it useful still to form his funeral pyre."

This epitaph on a seaman's tomb is ascribed to Plato :—

"I am a shipwrecked sailor's tomb: a peasant's there doth stand:
Thus the same world of Hades lies beneath both sea and land."

There are many more of the same class. This is by Poseidippus. The translation is nearly as given in Merivale's book, with the initials A. F. M. :—

"Oh, why, my brother-mariners, so near the boisterous wave
Of ocean have ye hollowed out my solitary grave?
'Twere better much that farther off a sailor's tomb should be,
For I dread my rude destroyer—I dread the roaring sea:
But may the smiles of fortune, and may love and peace await
All you who shed a pitying tear for poor Nicetas' fate."

On a shipwrecked person,—the translation by Mr Hodgson :—

"Perish the hour, that dark and starless hour—
Perish the roaring main's tempestuous power,
That whelmed the ship where loved Abdera's son
Prayed to unheeding Heaven, and was undone.
Yes—all were wrecked: and by the stormy wave
To rough Seriphus borne he found a grave—
Found from kind stranger hands funereal fires,
Yet reached, inurned, the country of his sires."

Here is another of the same class, ascribed to Plato, but on doubtful evidence :—

"Ye mariners, by sea and land be yours a happy doom;
But know, you now are sailing past a shipwrecked seaman's tomb."

This is by Leonidas :—

> "Fearless embark from the wrecked seaman's tomb:
> Others sailed safely when I met my doom."

This is by Callimachus, and exhibits his usual elegance. The translation is taken from Mr Symonds's book on the Greek Poets :—

> "Would that swift ships had never been; for so
>   We ne'er had wept for Sopolis: but he
> Dead on the waves now drifts; while we must go
>   Past a void tomb, a mere name's mockery."

There are one or two epitaphs upon slaves which are interesting, particularly as showing that the relation between a good master or mistress and a slave or perpetual bondsman was often friendly, and even affectionate. This is by Dioscorides :—

> "A slave, a Lydian, yet my master gave
>   To me, who fostered him, a freeman's grave:
> Master, live long; and when on life's decline
>   You come to Hades, there I'll still be thine."

This, by an anonymous author, in the same strain, is touching :—

> "Master, to thee still faithful I remain
> In death, and still my grateful thoughts retain;
> How, rescued thrice from fell disease by thee,
> I fill this cell, where passers-by may see
> Manes the Persian's tomb: for such good deed
> Service more true from all will be thy meed."

The next that we give is put into the mouth of another dying slave, also a Persian, bearing the name of a great river, and who deprecates any funeral rites that would be at variance with his creed:—

> "Burn not Euphrates, master; let not Fire
> Be here polluted for my funeral pyre.
> A Persian born, of Persia's genuine race,
> Fire to profane, to me were dire disgrace.
> Lay me in earth; nor even bring water here
> To wash me,—Rivers also I revere."

Manes, a name already mentioned, was commonly borne by slaves, and occurs in the following epigram by Anytè:—

> "Manes, when living, was a slave: dead now,
> Great King Darius, he's as great as thou."

This, on a female slave of high character, by Damaskios, will best bear translation in hexameters. It is not clear whether she had been manumitted during her lifetime:—

> "Zosima, who when alive was only a slave in the body,
> Now, in the body as well, freedom at last has obtained."

This chapter may be concluded by a few special epitaphs, real or supposed, upon persons of distinction. Of these perhaps the most celebrated, and certainly one of the best, is by Simonides, on Archedicè, the daughter of the Athenian tyrant Hippias, and wife of a tyrant's son at Lampsacus, where a monument was erected to her memory, on which the epitaph in question was actually inscribed:—

> "Of One who, high in Greece precedence held,
> Hippias, who all men of his day excelled,

> Archedicè the daughter here doth rest :
> Her father, brothers, husband, sons, possessed
> A princely rank ; but in her gentle mind
> None could a trace of arrogance e'er find."

Aristotle, who admired the genius and taste of Simonides, particularly refers to this epitaph as a specimen of judicious praise, the person mentioned being characterised as possessing that virtue which it was most difficult to practise in the position held by her. He gives as cases deserving of special eulogium when a prosperous person is moderate, or an unfortunate one magnanimous.

The next that we shall give is by Antipater of Sidon, upon Aristomenes, a Messenian prince, the determined enemy of Sparta, whose life, though undoubtedly historical, was adorned by exaggerations or additions of almost a legendary character. His chief qualities seem to have been patriotism, courage, and perseverance under difficulties, tempered with gentleness and tenderness of heart. A singular story is told of him,—that a Rhodian king, when consulting the Delphic oracle, was enjoined to marry the daughter of "the best of the Greeks." This he considered to be no other than Aristomenes, who thereafter found in Rhodes a peaceful refuge with his son-in-law. The epitaph which follows introduces upon the scene an eagle, by which bird his life had previously been saved when precipitated down a pit by the Spartans. The translation is by Leyden, and is very spirited :—

ON AN EAGLE PERCHED ON THE TOMBSTONE OF ARISTOMENES.

"Majestic Bird! so proud and fierce,
Why tower'st thou o'er that warrior's hearse?"
"I tell each god-like earthly king,
Far as o'er birds of every wing
Supreme the lordly eagle sails,
Great Aristomenes prevails.
Let timid doves, with plaintive cry,
Coo o'er the graves where cowards lie:
'Tis o'er the dauntless hero's breast
The kingly eagle loves to rest."

The advance and ultimate predominance of the Macedonian power over Greece proper, formed a tempting occasion to time-servers for flattering the conquerors. Some mortuary epigrams here occur as marking that era. The first we give is upon Philip of Macedon, by Addœus:—

"I, Philip, who first raised the Emathian name
By warlike deeds beyond all former fame,
Lie here at Ægæ: if you e'er shall see
One greater,—from my lineage it must be."

Ægæ was the place where the sepulchre of the Macedonian kings was situated. The allusion in the end is of course to Alexander the Great. Addœus was probably a Macedonian.

Connected with Philip's name is a very ungenerous epigram by Geminus, in honour of the Macedonian victories over the Athenians, and supposed to be inscribed upon a trophy:—

> "This stone to Mars must grief to Athens bring,
> Telling the might of Macedonia's king:
> The deeds of Marathon are now disgraced,
> The victories of Salamis effaced,
> Before the points of Philip's spears abased.
> Invoke the dead, Demosthenes; in vain!
> To taunt both quick and dead I here remain."

In one of his greatest speeches, Demosthenes had taken those who died at Marathon, and in other ancient battles, to witness that the resistance of the Athenians to Philip was laudable.

Here is a short complimentary epigram on Alexander's death, also by Addœus:—

> "Macetan Alexander's tomb, if called on to disclose,
> Say that the world's two continents his monument compose."

Macedonian is the word in the Greek, but the older adjective Macetan has been used, as more manageable.

Here is a later epigram by Parmenio, alluding to the story of the Pythian oracle having declared Alexander to be invincible:—

> "The rumour's false that Alexander's dead,
> Unless we hold that Phœbus told a lie:
> 'Thou art invincible,' the Pythian said;
> And those that are invincible can't die."

This is a tribute by Agathias to his sister, who to other accomplishments added the rather unusual one of a knowledge of Law, her brother's profession—the translation somewhat simplified:—

> "Bright Beauty, Music, legal Lore, Eugenia did adorn:
> Venus, the Muse, and Themis now for her their locks have shorn."

This is a beautiful dirge on some lovely and beloved object, said to be by Plato, and not unworthy of his name :—

"Aster, in life our Morning star, a lovely light you shed;
And now you shine as Hesperus, a star among the Dead."

We shall conclude this section, auspiciously, we hope, by a remarkable epitaph on a happy man. The name is not given, but the critics generally consider that the subject of it was a certain Quintus Metellus, mentioned by some minor historians, in whose case all the elements of good fortune concurred that are here enumerated. Carphyllides is the author :—

"View not my tomb with pity, passer-by:
No cause for tears o'er me, though doomed to die.
I've seen my children's children : a dear wife,
With me grown old, has cheered my lengthened life.
Three of my offspring, honourably wed,
Have given me grandsons from their fruitful bed,
Who in my lap have oft been lulled to sleep ;
For no disease or death e'er called to weep.
These, with due honours, blameless to my rest
Have sent me, in the region of the blest."

The Greek of the last phrase here used corresponds very closely to Lady Nairne's "Land of the leal."

CHAPTER IV.

AMATORY.

NOTWITHSTANDING the differences which exist in character and manners between the Greeks and ourselves, there could not fail to be a great community of feeling in the chief passions and affections of human nature. Both nations belong to one great and elevated family of the human race; neither of them can be considered as savage or barbarian, or other than highly civilised. Our languages have a great mutual affinity; and in some respects we stand aloof from other sections of humanity, whose institutions place them in a position essentially different from all European races. As regards the relation of the sexes, the great distinction arising from the presence or absence of polygamy is of itself enough to assimilate together those nations in which that source of female degradation does not exist. Faulty as Greek manners were, women were not treated as slaves or beasts of burden. The Greek matron was condemned to a certain seclusion, but she was held in respect; and in many cases, as we have already seen, the married life of the Greeks was one of affection and happiness.

Even the women that could not marry were not cruelly treated, and were not despised, except at least when they made an indiscriminate traffic of their attractions.

The sentiment of love must turn in varying degrees upon two elements — the appreciation of personal beauty, and the admiration or pleasure excited by mental powers of one kind or other. To both of these emotions the Greek mind was keenly alive, though in the young or the superficial the mental attraction which would exert the greatest influence would consist in the charm of conversational versatility, or in some of the more sociable and pleasurable accomplishments. These, we have seen, could in general be sought for only in those grades of the female sex which held an inferior status; but even with this class, amiable, though temporary, attachments might exist which would not be devoid of true affection. It should never be forgot that in men whose minds were of a higher and more serious order, a true and pure passion might exist towards superior women, of which there were not wanting remarkable examples. Ménage has an interesting treatise, dedicated to Madame Dacier, on the Female Philosophers of Greece; and many women there must have been who had great intellectual powers without being professed philosophers. It happens, besides, that our knowledge of the condition of Greek women is derived in a great degree from Athenian sources, referring thus to a locality where respectable females of Greek parentage were kept in closer seclusion than in other States.

The Greek amatory epigrams deal largely in mythological views. Venus and Cupid meet us at every turn; though Venus had other attributes than those which related to love.

This is a celebrated epigram upon Love—that is, Cupid—by Meleager:

"Dreadful is Love! dreadful! but where's the good
That oft this cry of 'dreadful' is renewed?
The urchin laughs at us; though o'er and o'er
Reproached, he's pleased; reviled, he thrives the more.
Venus, thou sea-born Queen! I much admire,—
Thou, sprung from water, shouldst produce this fire!"

One of the most beautiful of this class of epigrams —or it may be a fragment of a little poem which has found its way into the Anthology—is said to be by Plato, and presents a lovely picture of the god of Love laid asleep among roses, with the bees settling upon his lips:—

"We reached the grove's deep shadow, and there found
Cythera's son in sleep's sweet fetters bound,
Looking like ruddy apples on their tree:
No quiver and no bended bow had he;
These were suspended on a leafy spray.
Himself in cups of roses cradled lay,
Smiling in sleep; while, from their flight in air,
The brown bees to his soft lips made repair,
To ply their waxen task, and leave their honey there."

We shall have occasion to see that the Greeks had two Venuses whom they worshipped—one, the ordinary or Earthly, the other the Heavenly Venus. In like manner there were two Cupids corresponding to that distinction. There are epigrams in the Anthology referring specially to these several divinities. The following epigram on the Heavenly Cupid is ascribed to Marianus, and is quoted in Ogle's interesting book on 'Antiquities Explained,' where it is considered as illustrating a beautiful gem transmitted to us from antiquity. It does not seem certain that this is strictly the case; and we shall here insert the epigram independently, without special reference to the gem in question. The lines consist of a dialogue with Cupid, and sufficiently explain themselves. The translation is Ogle's own, a little altered :*—

"Where now thy pliant bow and subtle darts?
Those shafts that seek to pierce our inmost hearts?
Where now the wings that speed thy rapid flight?
Where now the torch that sheds a baneful light?
Why do those hands three flowery garlands bear?
And why a fourth restrain thy lovely hair?"
"Seek'st thou, good stranger, what I am to know?
To no corporeal source my birth I owe.
No gross material mother nursed my frame;
And all the Vulgar Venus I disclaim.
Men's souls by me to heavenly science rise,
And, fired with purer flames, possess the skies.
Four glorious wreaths my skilful hands entwine,
And Virtues four inspire the fair design.
Three of the garlands are about me spread,
And this, the wreath of Wisdom, binds my head."

The Earthly Cupid has a very different character; and the epigram that follows gives a lively and clever

* Ogle, p. 56.

account of his pedigree and peculiarities. It is by Meleager:—

"No wonder Cupid is a murderous boy,
  A fiery archer, making pain his joy.
His dam, while fond of Mars, is Vulcan's wife;
  And thus 'twixt fire and sword divides her life.
His mother's mother, too—why, that's the Sea!
  When lashed with winds, a roaring fury she.
No father has he, and no father's kin:
'Tis through the mother all his faults flow in.
Thus has he Vulcan's flames, the wild Sea's rage,
And Mars's blood-stained darts his wars on us to wage."

Here is a fanciful account of the first entry of love into a man's breast. Does it suggest that wine may often have something to do with it? It is by Julian the Egyptian, is a great favourite, and has often been translated:—

"Twining a wreath, I found, one day,
  Love, that among the roses lay;
Quick by the wings I caught him up,
  And plunged him in the brimming cup.
Then urged by thirst's imperious call,
  I drank the wine off, Love and all;
And ever since, within my breast,
  His tickling wings destroy my rest."

Here is one in which the connection between Love and Wine is directly pointed out. It is by Rufinus:—

"My breast is armed with Reason against Love:
  One against one, he shan't victorious prove.
Though I'm a mortal, an immortal he,
  Yet from the combat I will never flee.
But if he's joined by Bacchus, I'm undone:
  Who could resist such odds of two to one?"

We have already given several of Meleager's Sepulchral and Amatory epigrams; but it may now be convenient to add such others of his on the subject of Love as may best deserve our attention.

One of Meleager's favourite female friends bears the graceful name of Zenophilè—if indeed she was not a mere poetical creation, for the mistresses of poets have not always been real personages. We shall give some of the epigrams upon her without further introduction. The first, which describes the advent of spring, is translated by Professor Wilson himself, in a flowing and spirited style :—

" 'Tis now that the white violets steal out the spring to greet,
And that among his longed-for showers Narcissus smiles so sweet.
'Tis now that lilies, upland born, frequent the slopes of green,
And that the flower that lovers love, of all the flowers the queen,
Without an equal anywhere in full-blown beauty glows ;
Thou know'st it well, Zenophilè ! Persuasion's flower, the Rose.
Ah ! why, ye hills and meadows, does bright laughter thus illume
Your leafy haunts? so lavish why, and prodigal of bloom?
Not all the wreaths of all the flowers that Spring herself might cull
As mine own Virgin e'er could be one-half so beautiful ! "

The next, which celebrates the lady's musical powers, is translated by Mr Hay :—

"'Tis a sweet strain, by Pan of Arcady!
  Which warbles from thy lyre with thrilling sound,
Zenophilè. Oh! how can I be free,
  Since Loves on every side enclose me round,
Forbidding me to breathe a single hour
  In peace?—since first thy beauty, then thy lyre,
Thy grace, and then .... Oh! words of feeble power,
  Thy perfect *all* has set me all on fire."

Here is an epigram which it is supposed Ben Jonson may have had in view in writing his beautiful song, "Drink to me only with thine eyes:"—

"The wine-cup is glad: dear Zenophilè's lip
It boasts to have touched, when she stooped down to sip.
Happy wine-cup! I wish that, with lips joined to mine,
All my soul at a draught she would drink up like wine."

Among the Sepulchral epigrams has been given Meleager's beautiful lament upon Heliodora's death. We shall now insert one in an amatory strain, written before that sad event, if indeed it refers to the same Heliodora. There are many translations of it in the "Blackwood Papers," but we think it sufficient to select one by Wilson, in the same free and joyous spirit which his translations so often present:—

"I'll frame, my Heliodora! a garland for thy hair,
  Which thou, in all thy beauty's pride, mayst not disdain
      to wear;
For I, with tender myrtles, white violets will twine—
White violets, but not so pure as that pure breast of thine:
With laughing lilies I will twine narcissus; and the sweet
Crocus shall in its yellow hue with purple hyacinth meet:

And I will twine with all the rest, and all the rest above,
Queen of them all, the red red Rose, the flower which lovers love."

The following, which has been much admired, but has also occasioned some difficulty among critics, is translated by Mr Hay. It is an address by a lover who has come to the Hellespont, but is anxious to return to the island of Cos, the residence of Phanion, the object of his affection. He wishes the ships that are going southward to announce to the lady, if they should see her, his speedy return, and to inform her that when he is free he will not risk the dangers and delays of a sea-voyage, but will come to her on foot—an achievement not easily accomplished literally, as Cos is an island in the Ægean. But the proposal to come on foot may either be ascribed to the strength of the poet's imagination, or to the prosaic fact that if he came to the land nearest to Cos, there was but a short sea passage interposed :—

" Light barks of Helle's straits ! whose flagging sails
Woo the embraces of the northern gales,
If on the strand that views the Coan steep
You see my Phanion gazing on the deep,
' Thou beautiful !' say to her, ' these thy sighs
Hasten thy lover to thy longing eyes ;
Maiden beloved, I cannot wait the sea,
My eager feet will bring me soon to thee.'
Tell her these words, and Jove with favouring gales
Forthwith, at length, will fill your flagging sails."

We shall conclude our extracts from Meleager with two epigrams on Cupid which are well known, but which seem to be distinguished more for liveliness and ingenuity than for much beauty.

The first may be called the "Hue and Cry after Cupid"—a name which Ben Jonson has given to a very graceful masque embodying all the best ideas on the subject of the epigrammatists and other poets. Jonson's own poem has a proclamation beginning with this question:—

> "Beauties, have you seen this toy,
> Callèd Love, a little boy,
> Almost naked, wanton, blind,
> Cruel now, and then as kind?
> If he be among you, say:
> He is Venus' Runaway."

The whole of the poem is in the true Greek spirit, and deserves to be looked into. Of Meleager's "Hue and Cry" we give a translation by Merivale, noticing merely that Lesbia's name is substituted for Zenophilè's, as being shorter, for the rhythm's sake:—

> "Love, I proclaim, the vagrant child,
> Who, even now, at dawn of day,
> Stole from his bed and flew away.
> He's wont to weep, as though he smiled,
> For ever prattling, swift, and daring;
> Laughs with wide mouth and wrinkled nose;
> Wing'd on the back, and always bearing
> A quiver, rattling as he goes.
> Unknown the author of his birth;
> For Air, 'tis certain, ne'er begot
> The saucy boy; and as for Earth
> And Sea, both swear they own him not:
> To all and everywhere a foe.

But you must look and keep good watch,
Lest he should still around you throw
Fresh nets, unwary souls to catch.
Stay, while I yet am speaking, lo !
There, there he sits like one forbidden ;
And did you hope to 'scape me so—
In Lesbia's eyes, you truant, hidden ?"

The remaining epigram on Cupid relates to the proposal to sell the fugitive after he has been caught. The translation is by Mr Hay :—

" Sold he must be—there, while he lies asleep
On his own mother's breast ; I cannot keep
The bold, pert imp,—the jeering wingèd pest—
Whose active talons never are at rest.
The chattering, fearless creature, full of wiles,
With tearful eyes suffused, with roguish smiles,—
Eyes looking darts, whose glances all inflame,
Whose wildness even his mother cannot tame !
Sold he must be—the monster ;—buy him, pray,
Good stranger, only bear him far away.
Stop, stop, he weeps—sold, dear, thou shalt not be,
But dwell a pet with my Zenophilè."

We give now an epigram by Rufinus referring to a garland sent to Rhodoclèa, which may well match with Meleager's to Heliodora. The translation is by Mr Hay, but his last four lines have been condensed into two, which makes it correspond in length with the Greek original :—

" This crown of fairest flowers, my Rhodoclè,
Which my own hands have wreathed, I send to thee :
The lily,—the anemonè, moist with dew,
The rose, narcissus, and the violet blue.

> Thus crowned, let no vain thoughts thy mind invade,
> Thou, and the wreath, both bloom,—and both must fade."

We shall now add two more Love epigrams, by Rufinus, which exhibit considerable elegance:—

> "Where now Praxiteles? Where the skilful art
> Of Polycleitus, that could life impart?
> Who will mould Meletē's sweet-scented hair,
> Her lustrous eyes, her neck, like ivory fair?
> Sculptors and casters, sure we owe a shrine
> To her bright form as to a power divine."

Here is another, much admired and copied by several modern Latin poets:—

> "The eyes of Juno, Meletē, are thine,
> Minerva's hands, and Venus' breasts divine;
> While thy fair feet like Thetis' ankles shine.
> Happy is he who sees thee; he who hears
> Thy voice melodious, trebly blest appears:
> Who woos thee has a demigod's delight;
> And he who wins thee is immortal quite."

The feet of Thetis were particular objects of admiration, and "silver-footed" was her peculiar epithet. The last lines of the epigram remind one of Sappho's ode:—

> "Blest as the immortal gods is he,
> The youth that fondly sits by thee."

The next epigram that we shall give is by Agathias, and is often quoted, though perhaps it does not possess any high degree of excellence. The translation is by Mr Hay, a good deal altered:—

"The livelong night I spend in woe.
   And when the dawn appears,
That might bring rest to soothe my breast,
   And wipe away my tears ; .
These envious swallows haunt my door,
   With pipe so loud and shrill,
They will not leave me to repose,
   But twitter, twitter, still.
Ye chatterers, cease ; I did no harm
   To Philomela's tongue :
Go to the hoopoe's desert haunts,
   And there your woes prolong ;
And while you mourn poor Itys' fate,
   Perchance Rhodanthe's charms
May glow in dreams of blissful rest,
   Within these longing arms."

The story of Prognè, Philomela, Tereus, and Itys is too well known to require repetition here.

The ideas and images suggested by the passions or strong affections of humanity are wonderfully alike in various forms of society and literature. Nothing seems more natural than the utterance of the wishes of lovers to be transmuted into some object that will place them in proximity to the person beloved. Here are specimens from the Greek. The first is by Callistratus, who flourished in the second century B.C. It is translated, we think, by Merivale :—

"I wish I were an ivory lyre-
   A lyre of burnished ivory—
That to the Dionysian choir
   Blooming boys might carry me:

> Or would I were a chalice bright
> Of virgin gold by fire untried,
> For virgin chaste as morning light
> To bear me to the altar-side."

Imitated by Moore thus, in his collection of Epistles and Odes :—

> " If I were yonder conch of gold,
> And thou the pearl within it placed," &c.

This is by Anacreon, also translated by Merivale. After referring to the transmutation of Niobe and Progne, the poet continues :—

> " But I would be a mirror,
> So thou mayst pleas'd behold me ;
> Or robe, with close embraces
> About thy limbs to fold me ;
> A crystal fount, to lave thee ;
> Sweet oils, thy hair to deck ;
> A zone, to press thy bosom ;
> Or pearl, to gem thy neck :
> Or, might I worship at thy feet,
> A sandal for thy feet I'd be ;
> E'en to be trodden on were sweet,
> If to be trodden on by thee."

Here is another, also, we think, very beautiful. It is by some ascribed to Rufinus, by others to Dionysius the Sophist—while others, again, describe it as of uncertain parentage. Mr Merivale has translated it so far, but for some reason or other has omitted the last couplet as it appears in the Planudean Anthology. This we shall endeavour to supply, while we adopt Mr

Merivale's version as far as it goes, with a slight alteration to bring it nearer the original :—

> "Oh that I were some gentle air,
>   That when the heats of summer glow,
> And lay thy panting bosom bare,
>   I might upon that bosom blow!
> Oh that I were yon blushing rose,
>   Which even now thy hands have pressed,
> That I might love in sweet repose,
>   Reclining on thy snowy breast!
> Oh that I were a lily fair,
>   That, culled by fingers fairer still,
> I might thy every movement share,
>   And on thy beauty gaze my fill!"

See how modern feelings are apt to run, as Christopher North says, 'into the same sort of amorous fancy." Romeo in Shakespeare breathes the wish—

> "Oh that I were a glove upon that hand,
>   That I might touch that cheek!"

Christopher also appropriately refers to Burns :—

> "O that my love were yon red rose
>   That grows upon the castle wa',
> And I myself a drap o' dew,
>   Into her bonny breast to fa'!"
> O, there, beyond expression blest,
>   I'd feast on beauty a' the nicht,
> Sunk on her silk-saft faulds to rest,
>   Till fley'd awa' by Phœbus' licht."

Shakespeare, though no great scholar, had himself lived among profound and accomplished scholars. But Burns, we should think, knew little or nothing of the Greek anthologists; yet see how he fell into their style, and instinctively adopted their spirit. Here is another example. There is an anonymous Greek epigram which may be thus translated:—

> "Two evils, Poverty and Love,
>   My anxious bosom tear;
> The one my heart would little move,
>   But Love I cannot bear."

What is this but Burns's passionate lament?—

> "O poortith cauld, and restless love,
>   Ye wreck my peace between ye:
> But poortith a' I could forgie,
>   An' 'twerena for my Jeanie."

Again, the exquisite "Posie" of our Scottish bard equals and surpasses those garlands sent to their mistresses by Meleager and Rufinus, which we have above quoted. The truth is, that all these poets, Greek and British, had the same schoolmistress, Nature, who teaches her pupils a universal language.

Two or three smaller epigrams of this class may here be given. This is said to be by Plato:—

> "My star, thou view'st the stars on high:
> Would that I were that spangled sky,
> That I, thence looking down on thee,
> With all its eyes thy charms might see."

This is also ascribed to Plato, and it is certain that when a young man he wrote several amatory poems:—

> "My soul, love, on my lips, while kissing thee,
> Fluttered and longed to flit across from me."

This is by Capito :—

> "Beauty, on which no graces wait,
> May please, but not retain;
> Just as, without the barb, the bait
> Floats useless on the main."

This is by Asclepiades :—

"Sweet to the thirsty man is snow, to quench the summer's heat;
The winter's end, the spring's return, to sailors too is sweet;
But sweeter far when lovers twain have found a blissful bower,
Where mutual vows and mutual love will speed each happy hour."

This is anonymous :—

> "Venus, if men at sea you save,
> And rescue from the whelming wave,
> Me, too, a lover, I implore,
> Save from worse shipwreck here on shore."

This epigram, by Callimachus, was admired and paraphrased by Horace :—

> "The hunter, in the mountains, every roe,
> And every hare, pursues through frost and snow,
> Tracking their footsteps. But if some one say,
> 'See! here's a beast struck down,' he turns away.
> Such is *my* love: I chase the flying game,
> And pass with coldness the self-offering dame."

We may include in this chapter a fantastic epigram by Agathias on the loves of Venus and Anchises. Anchises in his old age still desires to testify his devotion to the goddess, and presents her with the only black hair he can find in his head, addressing her at the same time in these words :—

"Venus, thy spouse Anchises, whose young love
Oft drew thy footsteps to the Idæan grove,
Brings one dark hair, with difficulty found,
Sole relic of that age when joys abound.
Thou, goddess (for thou canst), his youth restore,
Or take grey hairs for what he was of yore."

Henry Stephens, for want, no doubt, of something better to do, gave 105 Latin translations of this last couplet.

We shall now conclude our amatory extracts with an epigram by Theocritus on the HEAVENLY VENUS :—

"Venus, but not the Vulgar one, you view :
Call her the Heavenly ; 'tis her title due.
Her image here Chrysogonè, the chaste,
Within the house of Amphicles has placed,
With whom a happy married life she led,
And many goodly children bore and bred.
Each rolling year was better than the past,
Flowing from thee, Divine One, first and last :
For they who gratefully the gods adore,
Still find their joys increasing more and more."

CHAPTER V.

DIDACTIC.

THE next class of epigrams on which we shall enter is the Didactic, or Gnomic, as they may be called—those, namely, that relate to the knowledge of life and duty, and which involve the maxims, precepts, or prudential rules by which our conduct may be guided. It deserves to be remembered that the dissemination of such truths and precepts was an early part of the system that led to inscriptional writings. Hipparchus, as we have already indicated, added to the more direct announcements of the Hermæ, or landmarks put up by him, a set of moral sentences for popular instruction; and some of these have been handed down to us. Here is an example. The original consisted of an hexameter and pentameter line. The hexameter on one side of the Hermes described the locality; the pentameter on the other set forth the name of the party erecting the image, with the moral precept meant to be inculcated—thus:

" This Hermes stands where Thria and the city's limits meet:
Hipparchus raised this monument: LET JUSTICE GUIDE YOUR FEET."

There is another, of which the first line is lost; the last is preserved:—

"The Deme of . . . here begins: the city's precincts end:
Hipparchus raised this monument: NEVER DECEIVE A FRIEND."

At a later period such precepts or truths would be inscribed anywhere, according to individual taste or fancy, wherever there was a vacant slab or an available pillar, on a summer-house or in a dwelling, as was done by the eccentric Englishman who put up the motto of "Waste not, want not" in his kitchen, not, probably, without some necessity for the admonition; and often such sayings would have no other existence than as literary efforts to be read or committed to memory, which their metrical form would facilitate.

One of the most excellent of this class of epigrams appears in the form of a model prayer by a pious and enlightened heathen, such as Socrates might be supposed to have preferred. It is anonymous:—

"Asked or unasked, things good, great Jove, supply:
Things evil, though we ask for them, deny."

This is like the prayer recommended by Juvenal in his celebrated tenth satire, and imported by Johnson into his "Vanity of Human Wishes:"—

"Still raise for Good the supplicating voice,
But leave to Heaven the measure and the choice."

Of special blessings to be desired, one of the most frequent is that of mediocrity of fortune: "Give me neither poverty nor riches." Here are some examples. The first is by Parmenio, translated by Mr Hay :—

> "Enough for me this cloak, though homely spun ;
> Fed on the flowers of song, your feasts I shun :
> I hate your wealthy fool—the flatterer's god—
> Nor hang I trembling on his awful nod :
> Calm and contented, I have learned to feel
> The blessed freedom of a humble meal."

Here is another by Alpheus of Mitylene, quaint, and often translated by Latin versifiers :—

> "I care not for those wide and fertile fields,
>   Nor all the wealth that Gyges held in fee :
> What joy a self-sufficing fortune yields,
>   Such modest livelihood is dear to me.
> The wise old maxim, 'Not too much '—
> Too much has power my heart to touch."

The just appreciation of wealth, and the knowledge of its true uses, is a favourite subject.

This is by Lucian, the translation partly by Hay :—

> "Enjoy your goods as if your death were near :
> Save them as if 'twere distant many a year.
> Sparing or spending, be thy wisdom seen
> In keeping ever to the golden mean."

Or thus :—

> "Wise is the man, prepared for either end,
> Who in due measure can both spare and spend."

This is upon a miser, anonymous :—

> "All say that you are rich : I say, Not so :
> You're poor : wealth only by its use we know.
> What you enjoy is yours : what for your heirs
> You hoard, already is not yours but theirs."

This is by Paul the Silentiary, translated by Hay:—

"No gracious boon is life, if vexing cares
Wither the temples with thin hoary hairs
Be mine *enough*—since too much golden store
Always corrodes the maddened heart the more.
Thence better oft, amid this mortal strife,
Is poverty than riches, death than life.
Since thus it is, on Wisdom fix thy gaze;
Hers thy heart's wishes, hers be all its ways."

This, again, is upon a miser, by Lucillius:—

"Yours is a pauper's soul, a rich man's pelf:
Rich to your heirs, a pauper to yourself."

The transitory nature of property is thus depicted by an unknown writer. A field is personified as speaking:—

"Once I was Achæmenides's field:
He to Menippus now his claim must yield.
Thus I for ever pass from hand to hand,
And each possessor thinks me his own land.
All of them think so; but they all are wrong;
To none, but Fortune only, I belong."

The following reflection upon the succession of heirs, said to be by Simonides, is to the same effect:—

"My heir rejoices when I die; and so
His heir will do, when he in turn shall go:
This debt we all of us to nature owe."

It is a great question whether life on the whole is happy or the reverse. Archias, who, without being original, is often elegant, commends the Thracians for their views in this respect. The translation is a little altered from Hay's, and a couplet borrowed from Bland has been added :—

"Praiseworthy are the Thracians, who lament
　The infant that hath left its mother's womb :
Who deem those happy, too, whom Death has sent
　Without prevision to the peaceful tomb.
Well in their grief and gladness is express'd
That Life is labour, and that Death is rest."

Two epigrams are well known as advocating opposite views of human life,—the one maintaining that no course or career is satisfactory, and that, as Silenus was said to have taught, it is better either to have never been born, or immediately to die; the other, that every path or position in life has its advantages, and that life on the whole is a boon and a source of enjoyment.

The epigram against Life is by Posidippus, or, as some say, Crates. The translation is by Hay :—

"Which the best way of life ? The forum rings
With bickering brawls ; home, too, vexation brings :
Toil in the country, terror reigns at sea :
Abroad wealth trembles lest its goods may flee ;
And want is woe : trouble, thy name is wife :
A single is a solitary life :
Children are cares ; cheerless a childless state :
Youth is but folly ; weak a hoary pate.
Since thus it is, a wise man still should cry
Ne'er to be born, or being born to die."

The opposite side of the argument is maintained by Metrodorus, the translation slightly altered from Hay's :—

"Good all the ways of life : the forum rings
 With deeds of glorious enterprise ; home brings
 Sweet rest ; the charms of Nature clothe the fields;
 The sea brings gain : abroad wealth honour yields :
 Want may be hid ; comfort, thy name is wife :
 A single is a free and easy life.
 Children are joys : cares shun the childless bed :
 Strength attends youth ; reverence the hoary head.
 Since thus it is, a wise man's choice should be,
 Both to be born, and born such good to see."

Whether life on the whole be a success or a failure, there can be no doubt that it is uncertain, both in its tenure and duration, and that at the best its enjoyments are fleeting and perishable. Hear, on this subject, a strain from our old friend Simonides, though it is liker an elegy than an epigram. The translation we give is by Merivale :—

"All human things are subject to decay :
 And well the man of Chios tuned his lay—
 'Like leaves on trees the race of man is found ;'
 Yet few receive the melancholy sound,
 Or in their breasts imprint this solemn truth,
 For hope is near to all, but most to youth.
 Hope's vernal season leads the laughing hours
 And strews o'er every path the fairest flowers :
 To cloud the scene, no distant mists appear ;
 Age moves no thought, and death awakes no fear.
 Ah ! how unmindful is the giddy crowd
 Of the small span to youth and life allowed !
 Ye who reflect, the short-lived good employ ;
 And while the power remains, indulge your joy."

Some of this translation is too free ; and to the four

lines beginning "Hope's vernal season," we should prefer the following, as closer to the original :—

"While the light heart the joys of youth deceive,
We dream of things we never can achieve.
Age moves no thought, and death awakes no fear:
Nor look we for disease while health is here."

This is by Lucian :—

"Things owned by mortals needs must mortal be,
Away our best possessions from us flee;
And if at times they seem disposed to stay,
Then *we* from *them* too quickly flee away."

This is anonymous :—

"Short is the rose's bloom; another morn
Will show no rose, but, in its stead, a thorn."

Regarding life as thus uncertain and transitory, the great question comes to be, in what manner it shall best be passed, so as to secure the blessings which it is capable of yielding. Two opposite views on this subject will always be taken by different schools of thought and morals. Labour and virtue will be the resources of the one, and pleasure and self-indulgence of the other. Simonides, we are glad to say, will be found here to have chosen the better part, though now and then he may seem to relax the strictness of his tone. His fragment upon Virtue is worthy of all praise. The translation we give is partly borrowed from Mr Hay :—

"'Tis said that Virtue dwells sublime
On rugged cliffs, full hard to climb,

> Where round her ranged, a sacred band
> Acknowledge her divine command ;
> But mortal ne'er her form may see,
> Unless his restless energy
> Breaks forth in sweat that gains the goal,
> The perfect manhood of the soul."

The allusion to "sweat" as the outward token of generous exertion is frequent in the best Greek poets. Thus Hesiod, as translated by Elton :—

> "Where Virtue dwells, the gods have placed before
> The dropping *sweat* that springs from every pore,
> And ere the feet can reach her bright abode,
> Long, rugged, steep the ascent, and rough the road.
> The ridge once gained, the path so hard of late
> Runs easy on, and level with the gate."

The two following epigrams may also be referred to. They purport to contain the words that "Juno would have spoken," when Hercules on his deification was admitted to Olympus. They are both anonymous :—

> "Now, Hercules, your virtue's generous sweat
> Has from your sire this bright requital met ·
> After its round of conflicts, labour gains
> Unbounded honour to reward its pains."

> "Labour and mighty sweat have for you gained
> This grace, a seat in heaven, by none before attained."

Another epigram by Onestes has a close resemblance to some of those we have just quoted :—

> "You toiled up Helicon ; but nectar, poured
> From the Pegasian well, your strength restored :
> So Wisdom's path is steep ; but, gained the height,
> The Muses' gifts will fill you with delight."

It should be observed that in classical writers the Muses do not represent, as they often do with us, the powers of poetry or even of literature only, but embrace the whole range of the sciences, including physical science. Thus Virgil, in his Second Georgic, describing the objects of his ambition, speaks in these terms :—

"Ye sacred Muses! with whose beauty fired
My soul is ravished and my brain inspired,
Whose priest I am, whose holy fillets wear,
Would you your poet's first petition hear,
Give me the ways of wandering stars to know,
The depths of heaven above, and earth below," &c.

This that follows is a noble strain in praise of Equanimity, by Archilochus, which we here give, though his era is earlier than that of the proper epigrammatists. The translation is Mr Hay's, somewhat altered :—

"Toss'd on a sea of troubles, Soul, my Soul,
  Thyself do thou control ;
And to the weapons of advancing foes
  A stubborn breast oppose ;
Undaunted 'mid the hostile might
Of squadrons burning for the fight.

Thine be no boasting, when the victor's crown
  Wins thee deserved renown ;
Thine no dejected sorrow, when defeat
  Would urge a base retreat :
Rejoice in joyous things—nor overmuch
  Let grief thy bosom touch
'Midst evil, and still bear in mind,
How changeful are the ways of humankind."

Let us add one or two more of these high-minded compositions.

This is a versification of a celebrated thought expressed by Thales; it is by Lucian :—

"Committing wrong, the chance may be that you elude
    men's eyes ;
You never can elude the gods, when wrong you e'en
    devise."

What follows is said to be the precept of a Pythian oracle :—

"Cleansed in thy soul, enter the holy place
    Of the pure god, touching the lustral wave;
The good need little water, but the base
    Free from their guilt not ocean's self can lave."

The contemplation of death is necessarily in its various aspects present to the minds of all thinking men, and there are many Greek epigrams upon it,—some of them dealing with it in a high and noble spirit, and others seeking to use it chiefly as an incentive to present enjoyment. It is not every one of our pagan friends who realised the wise wish of Martial, that he might always be able

"To look on life with placid eye,
    And neither fear nor wish to die."

But the Greek poets were not generally cowards in this matter. This by Agathias is a fair specimen. The version is chiefly taken from Bland :—

"Why fear ye death, the parent of repose,
    That puts an end to penury and pain?

His presence once, and only once, he shows,
   And none have seen him e'er return again.
But maladies of every varying hue
In thick succession human life pursue."

Æschylus had anticipated this last idea by writing of death as the only "healer of irremediable ills."

The following epigram by Æsopus takes a somewhat similar view of death as a remedy. The translation is by Dr Wellesley:—

"From thee, O life! and from thy myriad woes,
Who but by death can flee or find repose?
For though sweet Nature's beauties gladden thee,
The sun, the moon, the stars, the earth, the sea,
All else is fear and grief; and each success
Brings its retributive unhappiness."

We are not indiscriminately fond of Palladas's epigrams, though Erasmus is said to have admired them. Some of them are repulsive; but the following, though exaggerated, aims at a higher tone. It is uncertain whether Palladas was a Christian:—

"The Body is a torture to the Soul;
A hell, a fate, a load, a stern control,
That weighs it to the ground with many woes,
Nor e'er allows it to enjoy repose.
But from the Body, as from Death, set free,
It flies to God and Immortality."

We shall here insert another by Palladas as to the advantages of the mediocrity of fortune:—

"Envy, as Pindar has averred,
   To Pity should be much preferred:
The envied have a brilliant fate;
Pity is given where griefs are great.

> But I would wish alike to be
> From pity and from envy free.
> A mean is best: high places know
> Great perils: scorn still haunts the low.

Many of the epigrammatists, it must be confessed, make the shortness and uncertainty of life and the certainty of death an argument for conviviality. Exhortations such as we are now to introduce are common. The first one is anonymous; the translation compounded from Bland and Wellesley:—

> "Drink and be glad: to-morrow what may be,
> Or what thereafter, none of us can see.
> Haste not nor fret: but now as well's you may,
> Feast and be merry; freely give away;
> Remember joys can last but with the breath,
> And think how short a space parts life and death;
> An instant:—seize what good may now befall;
> Dead, thou hast nothing, and another all."

This, to the same effect, is by Palladas; the version is partly Hay's:—

> "To die is due by all: no mortal knows
> Whether to-morrow's dawn his life may close.
> Knowing this well, O man, let cheering wine,
> That sweet forgetfulness of death, be thine.
> Give way to love too: live from day to day,
> And yield to Fate o'er all things else the sway."

This next remonstrance obviously comes from a voluptuary, who, besides thinking a bird in the hand worth two in the bush, prefers that any expensive offerings should be given when he can feel the good of them, rather than when he is incapable of doing so. It is anonymous—the translation by Merivale:—

> "Seek not to glad these senseless stones
>   With fragrant ointments, rosy wreaths;
> No warmth can reach our mouldering bones
>   From lustral fire that vainly breathes.
> Now let me revel whilst I may:
>   The wine that o'er my grave is shed
> Mixes with earth and turns to clay:
>   No honours can delight the dead."

We may here advert to a practice that seems to have been observed in Greece, connected with the feelings which we are describing, and which presents a melancholy and to Christian minds a miserable feeling. The Greeks, it is generally thought, did not use skeletons and death's-heads as funeral emblems, but rather represented death on their monuments under the form of Sleep, in the act often of extinguishing a torch. But they did use, or at least the voluptuaries among them used, the more painful reminiscences of death as incentives to social indulgences. A very singular epigram has been preserved illustrating this practice. It is by Polemo, and seems to refer to some gem or ornament of a convivial tendency; and, indeed, the last couplet is said to have been found inscribed on a gem:—

> "The poor man's armour see! this flask and bread,
> This wreath of dewy leaves to deck the head;
> This bone, too, of a dead man's brain the shell,
> The Soul's supreme and holy citadel.
> The carving says, 'Drink, eat, and twine your flowers;
> This dead man's state will presently be ours.'"

Herodotus tells us that the old Egyptians at their

banquets used to send round a wooden form of a skeleton with this exhortation—"Looking upon this, drink and enjoy yourself; for when you are dead you will be like this." Plutarch says of this custom that though it was unseemly, yet it had this use, " to incite the spectators not to luxury and drunkenness, but to mutual love and friendship,"—which is, to say the least, somewhat doubtful.

We are afraid that, upon the whole, temperance in the use of wine was not a conspicuous virtue among the Greeks, or at least among the Athenians. Their tendency to indulgence in this respect may be inferred not merely from their dramatists and miscellaneous writers, but also from the philosophical accounts of their Symposia, as represented by Plato and Xenophon, though they seem to have submitted to certain restraints of a rather peculiar kind. There was an idea that drinking was not generally allowable to young men, but was a privilege of the old, who needed it more ; and Socrates in Plato lays it also down as a medical rule that drinking should not take place on two consecutive evenings. The conversations, of course, would vary according to the character of the guests ; but if Plato's writings are to be held as founded on fact, it is clear that very late and long sittings must have been thus spent. Such excesses were all the more likely to take place, and to become exaggerated, from the exclusion of women from their feasts ; and when once established, the conversational propensities of the Greeks, or at least of the Athenians, would make them frequent and favourite **enjoyments.**

The customs of different countries in these respects are well worth observing. Probably the French, of all other nations, most nearly approach to the Greeks in conversational powers and propensities; but the forms of French society and some of their national virtues, their courtesy to women, and their habitual temperance, led to this result, that the drawing-rooms or ladies' apartments were the ordinary scenes of their conversational displays, and that women not only held their own part but took the lead in these *réunions*. On the other hand, English ladies have their share of conversation, but a peculiarity exists in English society little known elsewhere. Talleyrand, we believe, expressed the opinion that the half-hour, more or less, passed by men in England over their wine, after the ladies have left the dinner-table, is an important adjunct to the British constitution. Englishmen seem to need some wine to brighten their faculties; when left alone in this way they can talk freely on all public subjects without mixing up ladies with politics, and a tone, it is thought, is attained, among political thinkers, of moderation, courtesy, and mutual forbearance, eminently conducive to that most important object, the predominance of good sense and sound judgment in all public matters.

The freedom of conviviality adopted and enjoined by the Greeks may be seen in some of their popular sayings; and among others, in the proverb which denounced as a nuisance any bottle-companion that has "a good memory." This idea is vigorously expanded in the following epigram by Antipater:—

"Not the setting of the Pleiades so fearful is to me,—
Not the howling round the rugged rock of a wild and
    stormy sea,—
Not the flash that fires the mighty heavens,—as the water-
    drinking fellow,
Who remembers and repeats the things we said when we
    were mellow."

We suspect we must hold that both Plato and Xenophon come, strictly speaking, under the censure of being convivial companions who "remember and repeat" what passes at wine-parties; for many of their reminiscences relate to scenes where wine has had a good deal to do with the conversation; but the world will not regret that in this respect they should have transgressed the rule imposed on ordinary convivialities.

It ought here to be mentioned that the character of the Greek wine generally was such that all but the grossly intemperate diluted it largely with water. Even the mixture of *half-and-half* was thought too strong. Several epigrams contain allusions to this subject. This is by Meleager. The nymphs are the impersonation of water:—

"Bacchus, from Semelè's scorched body saved,
    The Nymphs received, and with pure water laved.
    Hence he and they are friends: if you decline
    To let them mix, you'll swallow fire for wine."

Carousals were generally conducted according to some method prescribed or enforced by a chosen president or symposiarch, as he was called. The great distinction was whether the drinking should be compulsory or optional as to quantity, men of sense of course preferring the voluntary system. This is illustrated by the following epigram by Onestes :—

> "Freedom in drinking always is the best:
> Force is an insult to both wine and guest.
> Some *on* the ground their wine will slily pour;
> Some *under* ground may sink to Lethe's shore.
> Away, ye sots! the needs of natural joy
> A modest measure amply will supply."

We do not think it necessary to lay before our readers more of these convivial verses, or to give them any of the Anacreontic class, with which most people must be familiar in some shape or other. The best imitation in English of the Anacreontic style is perhaps to be found in Cowley's smaller poems.

This section may be concluded by a few miscellaneous epigrams on general life and manners.

The first we give is a fanciful supplication to two of our faculties, by Macedonius. It reminds us of the saying of Themistocles, when Simonides proposed to teach him Mnemonics, or the art of memory, that he would rather learn the art of forgetfulness :—

> "Memory, and thou, Forgetfulness, all hail!
> Each in her province greatly may avail.
> Memory, of all things good remind us still:
> Forgetfulness, obliterate all that's ill."

This is a kind of counterpart, by the same author :—

> "Memory, and thou, Forgetfulness, not yet
> Your powers in happy harmony I find:
> *One* oft recalls what I would fain forget,
> And *one* blots out what I would bear in mind."

This, which is anonymous, embodies the well-known saying of Anaxagoras, that every place is at the same distance from the infernal regions:—

> "Straight the descent to Hades, whencesoe'er,
> From Athens or from Meroé, you fare:
> Nor grieve to die when far from home; you'll find
> To Hades everywhere a favouring wind."

The next is by Lucillius:—

> "I mourn not those who lose their vital breath;
> But those who, living, live in fear of death."

This is by Palladas:—

> "Father of flatterers, Gold, of Pain and Care begot,
> A fear it is to have thee, and a pain to have thee not."

This, again, is by Lucillius:—

> "If one grown old still longer life implores,
> I wish his years prolonged for many scores."

This is by Theognis:—

> "Woe's me for joyful youth, and joyless eld!
> This coming, I behold; that going, I've beheld."

The next is by Philo:—

> "Grey hairs are wisdom—if you hold your tongue:
> Speak—and they are but hairs, as in the young."

This is by Lucian:—

> "The happy think a lifetime a short stage:
> One night to the unhappy seems an age."

This, upon deliberation and rashness, is by the same:—

> "Slow-footed Counsel is most sure to gain;
> Rashness still brings Repentance in her train."

Give quickly, if you give at all, is thus recommended by an anonymous writer:—

> "Swift kindnesses are best: a long delay,
> In kindness, takes the kindness all away."

This, too, is anonymous:—

> "Too much is always bad: old proverbs call
> Even too much honey nothing else than gall."

This next, which is also anonymous, requires some explanation, as it turns upon the letters of the Greek alphabet:—

> "Six hours suffice for work: when these we give,
> The next four letters order us to 'live.'"

It has been a common amusement for studious men to expand this epigram by a more minute subdivision of time. In Sir Edward Coke's Diary there is a Latin triplet on the subject, of which Mr Amos, in his interesting 'Gems of Latin Poetry,' tells us that he found this version upon a fly-leaf of an old law-book:—

> "Six hours to sleep allot: to law be six addressed:
> Pray four: feast two: the Muses claim the rest."

Sir William Jones tried to improve this by rather too quaint a conceit, thus:—

> "Seven hours to law; to soothing slumber seven:
> Ten to the world allow; and *all* to Heaven."

His couplet had been misquoted, and Mr Amos points out an unmeaning dispute between Croker and Macaulay on the basis of that false reading.*

---

* Amos, Gems, p. 120.

These modern compositions are all obviously founded upon the Greek epigram above given, but of which the essential part cannot be seen in a translation. The turning-point of it lies here, that the letters of the Greek alphabet, with the addition of three other signs, are used as numerals; and when you have expressed the *six* hours in that way, the next *four* letters are these—z, ē, th, i, which, when put together, make the imperative mood of the verb *to live*. To live, we suspect, may have a good many different meanings. "To live and love" is a phrase of Catullus; but the best view of the epigram is to suppose that "living" here embraces all the employments and enjoyments of life that will enable us better to labour when the season of labour returns. We find it thus expanded in a stray MS. found in a folio Anthology :—

"Six hours are due to labour, and no more:
 Count these in letters, and the following *four*
 Tell man to 'live:' to eat and drink and play,
 And sleep and wake, and think, and watch and pray."

The following is an epigram by Macedonius, giving a very liberal view of the duties of hospitality, a virtue particularly necessary in certain states of society, and not inappropriate in a pretty wide sense in some remote parts even of our own country :—

"Stranger and countryman to me
 Welcome alike shall ever be.
 To ask of any guest his name,
 Or whose he is, or whence he came,
 I hold can never be *his* part
 Who owns a hospitable heart."

The following is a eulogium on the value of friendship, anonymous:—

"A good friend's a great treasure, Heliodorus,
As great as any Heaven can set before us:
At least to him to whom 'tis also given
To keep, when he has got, that gift of Heaven."

Here is an ingenious recommendation to secure the friendship of an affectionate woman, by Antipater:—

"Me, a dry plane-tree now, a clustering vine
Envelops: this fair foliage is not mine.
Yet once I nursed her fruit with many a bough,
As verdant and as fresh as she is now.
Do thou thus strive to gain a woman's love,
Who to thy dying day will grateful prove."

We may conclude this section with a sententious enumeration of the Seven Wise Men of Greece, which, as it is rather like doggerel in the Greek, can scarcely appear better in the translation. It is anonymous:—

"I'll tell the names and sayings and the places of their birth,
Of the Seven great ancient Sages, so renowned on Grecian earth:
The Lindian Cleobulus said—'The mean was still the best:
The Spartan Chilo, 'Know thyself,' a heav'n-born phrase confessed:
Corinthian Periander taught, 'Our anger to command:'
'Too much of nothing,' Pittacus, from Mitylene's strand:
Athenian Solon this advised, 'Look to the end of life:'
And Bias from Prienè showed, 'Bad men are the most rife:'
Milesian Thales urged that 'None should e'er a surety be:'
Few were their words, but, if you look, you'll much in little see."

CHAPTER VI.

LITERARY AND ARTISTIC.

The next class of epigrams to be noticed consists of the Literary and Artistic, which often run into each other, and may therefore be embraced in the same section, although they admit of a certain degree of separation.

LITERARY.

The epigrams upon poets may begin the list. It has been supposed that these epigrams, which are very numerous, had—many of them at least—originally formed a continuous poem, exhibiting a gallery of the successive poets thus celebrated. This may to a certain extent have been the case, particularly as a considerable number of these epigrams are by the same author—Antipater of Sidon. But that circumstance is not conclusive; there are a great many other epigrams by other authors, and they descend to us certainly as detached compositions.

There come here, in the first place, two upon Orpheus. The following is by Antipater; the translation partly from the versions of Bland and Hay:—

"No longer, Orpheus, will thy soothing song,
  Oaks, rocks, and lawless monsters lead along:
No longer lull the stormy winds to sleep;
The hail, the drifting snow, the raging deep.
Thou'rt gone; the Muses weep around thy bier,
And most, Calliope, thy mother dear.
Why mourn our children lost, when from the grave
The gods themselves cannot their offspring save!"

The next is anonymous. The Thracian women, in a fit of frenzy, had put Orpheus to death, but now lamented him with all the tokens of repentance:—

"Orpheus, now dead,—Calliope's, and high Œagrus' son,—
The fair-haired Thracian women wept, rueing the deed thus done:
Their arms they lanced with weapons keen, till the blood freely flowed,
And o'er their locks, in sign of grief, were dust and ashes strowed.
The Muses, too, with the bright god who bears the heavenly lyre,
Burst into tears and tuneful sighs—a melancholy choir,
Mourning their much-loved minstrel much; while rocks and trees around
Added their wail for him whose harp had soothed them with its sound."

Homer comes next, on whom there is here an epigram by Antiphilus, translated by Mr Hay. It is in the form of a dialogue between Antiphilus and the Iliad and Odyssey:—

Antiphilus. Who are ye, Books, and what do ye contain?
Books. Daughters of Homer we, and we explain
The tale of Troy, Achilles' wrath, the might
Of Hector's struggle in the ten years' fight,

Ulysses' toils, the tears his consort shed,
The wooers' struggles for her widowed bed.
 Antiphilus. Great Works, go join the Muses' choir in heaven,
For Time proclaims their number now eleven.

This is by Leonidas of Tarentum :—

" The fiery sun, when wheeling up heaven's height,
 Obscures the stars and the moon's holy light ;
So Homer, seen 'mid the poetic throng,
 Dims by his splendour all the orbs of song."

Every one knows the verses—

" Seven Grecian cities vied for Homer dead,
 Through which the living Homer begged his bread ;"

a tradition which doubtless suggested to Horace Smith the supposition, that his Egyptian mummy might in his day " have dropped a halfpenny in Homer's hat." The seven cities have been differently enumerated in different epigrams, but this couplet will give one edition of them :—

" Seven cities vied for Homer's birth, with emulation pious,
 Salamis, Samos, Colophon, Rhodes, Argos, Athens, Chios."

Antipater will have it that this uncertainty is easily explained and easily solved. The translation is Merivale's :—

" From Colophon some deem thee sprung ;
 From Smyrna some, and some from Chios ;
These noble Salamis have sung,
 While *those* proclaim thee born in Ios ;
And others cry up Thessaly,
 The mother of the Lapithæ.

> Thus each to Homer has assigned
> The birthplace just which suits his mind;
> But if I read the volume right,
> By Phœbus to his followers given,
> I'd say they're all mistaken quite:
> His real country must be Heaven;
> While for his mother—She can be
> No other than Calliope."

There are many more epigrams upon Homer, but we must make a selection.

This is by Philippus the Anthologist. It is somewhat commonplace:—

> "Sooner shall heaven put out the stars—the night
> Be gilded by the sun's resplendent light;
> The sea to men a pleasant beverage yield,
> Or the dead rise to range Life's busy field,
> Than blank forgetfulness shroud Homer's name,
> And of those ancient pages quench the fame."

Another, by Alcæus of Messene, is founded on the tradition that Homer died on the island of Ios, and that his death was occasioned or hastened by his inability to solve a foolish riddle propounded to him by some fisher lads, against which catastrophe, it is said, he had been warned by an oracle. The story of the riddle is beneath contempt, though riddles, from the time of the Sphinx, were serious things, as may also appear from the Scripture story of Samson. The translation is by Mr Hay, a little altered :—

> " Sorely afflicted was the hero's bard,
> When Ios' sons devised that riddle hard:
> Upon their Homer's corse the Nereids pour
> Nectar, when stretched upon its cliffy shore;

> For he had honoured Thetis and her son,
> With other heroes who had glory won,
> And told the deeds by wise Ulysses done.
> Ios, though small, most blest of Isles! since he,
> The Muses and the Graces' star, now sleeps in thee!"

This that follows is by Alpheus of Mitylene :—

> " Still of Andromachè the wail we hear,
>   Still see Troy's ramparts tottering to the ground;
> The din, where Ajax fights, still strikes the ear,
>   And steeds drag Hector's corse the walls around,
> Through Homer's Muse, whom not one land alone,
> But climes of either world proclaim their own."

Several of the other epigrams upon Homer have a connection probably with those feelings which ultimately came to pay him divine honours, and which culminated in that wonderful work of art, the Apotheosis of Homer, now preserved among the Townley Sculptures in the British Museum.* Here is an epigram upon a statue of Homer erected at Argos—the author anonymous :—

> " This is the god-like Homer; he who, fraught
> With wisest words, to Greece high glory brought:
> And most to Argives, who the god-built Troy
> Did for fair Helen's crime by force destroy.
> Grateful to him their city here has placed
> His image, and with heavenly honours graced."

The next epigram, which is anonymous, seems to point directly to a kind of apotheosis :—

> " If Homer is a god, let worship due be given;
> If he is not a god, then think him now in heaven."

---

* See ' Handbook to the Antiquities of the British Museum,' in which a woodcut of this beautiful bas-relief is given.

What follows belongs to that class of epigrams of which there are many in the Anthology, with the title, "What words some one would have said as to some particular person or occasion." It is put into the mouth of Apollo:—

> "I sang those songs that gained so much renown:
> I Phœbus; Homer merely wrote them down."

Our next epigram is rather an extravagant piece of jocularity:—

> "Homer so sang of Troy destroyed by fire,
> That envy seized the towns that stood entire."

This is upon Hesiod, by Asclepiades or Archias; the translation by Goldwin Smith:—

> "The Muses, Hesiod, on the mountain steep,
> Themselves at noon thy flocks beheld thee keep;
> The bright-leaved bay they plucked, and all the Nine
> Placed in thy hand at once the branch divine.
> Then their dear Helicon's inspiring wave,
> From where the wing'd steed smote the ground, they gave,
> Which deeply quaffed, thy verse the lineage told
> Of gods, and husbandry, and heroes old."

The next poet to be noticed is Archilochus, a writer of wonderful reputation among the ancients, but of whom we have only a few fragments, full of a sublime energy enough to convince us of the character and spirit of what we have lost. He was born of a noble family at Paros, whence he emigrated in his youth to Thasos, at the time when a colony of Parians was founded in that place. "He was," says Professor Wilson, "among the first, and by far the greatest, of soldier-poets;" "yet on the field of battle he left behind his shield,"—an incident which he sought to gloss over by writing the following epigram, of which we give Merivale's translation:—

> "The foeman glories o'er my shield—
> I left it on the battle-field:
> I threw it down beside the wood,
> Unscathed by scars, unstained with blood.
> And let him glory: since from death
> Escaped, I keep my forfeit breath,
> I soon may find at little cost
> As good a shield as that I've lost."

He was a fearful satirist, and there is a strange story of his having driven to suicide the daughters of Lycambes by a lampoon, in revenge for some slight or injury received from one of them, his betrothed or his wife, Neobulè.

Epigrams upon him are to be found, sometimes laudatory and sometimes the reverse. We begin with one in his praise by Leonidas or Theocritus. The translation is founded on a very poor one by Fawkes, which it is not easy to raise above mediocrity:—

> "Stand, and Archilochus, the bard, behold!
> Him, by his keen iambics known of old:
> Whose glory has by myriad pathways run
> To realms of night and to the rising sun.
> The Muses much their zealous votary loved;
> And Phœbus, too, on him his favour proved:
> Where care and skill were matched with equal fire,
> Fit strains to frame and sing them to his lyre."

The next will show the reverse of the medal:—

> " Archilochus's seaside tomb you see,
>   Who first with viperous gall stained poesie,
>   Wounding sweet Helicon—Lycambes knew
>   Its fury well, when 'twas his fate to view
>   Three strangled daughters whom this slanderer slew.
>   Pass softly, stranger, lest it be your doom
>   To wake the wasps that settle on his tomb."

There are more of the same kind, but the subject is not a pleasant one. One view, however, in an epigram of a lighter kind, suggests that if he had not taken to satire, he might have rivalled the greatest of poets :—

> " Here lies Archilochus, whom the Muse impelled
>   To fierce iambics, that with venom swelled :
>   Lest her dear Homer she should see excelled."

The next of the poets in order seems to be Sappho, on whom there are several epigrams.

This is by Antipater :—

> " Sappho my name, in song o'er women held
>   As far supreme, as Homer men excelled."

The next is by Pinytus :—

> " This tomb reveals where Sappho's ashes lie,
>   But her sweet words of wisdom ne'er will die."

This, again, is by Antipater, translated by Wellesley :—

> " Amazement seized Mnemosyné
>   At Sappho's honey'd song :
>   'What, does a tenth Muse, then,' cried she,
>   'To mortal men belong !' "

Here is another, anonymous :—

> "Come, Lesbian maids, to blue-eyed Juno's grove,
> With steps that lightly o'er the entrance move.
> There to the goddess form a graceful dance,
> While Sappho as your leader shall advance,
> Bearing her golden lyre. With her rejoice!
> Her song will seem Calliope's own voice."

This is ascribed to Plato :—

> "Some thoughtlessly proclaim the Muses nine,
> A tenth is Lesbian Sappho, maid divine."

Coupled with Sappho's name, and next hers in order, we sometimes meet with that of Erinna, but there is not sufficient ground for assigning to that poetess so early a date. She was obviously, however, a favourite with the epigrammatists, and seems to deserve her reputation, though we have not enough of her poetry preserved to enable us fully to appreciate her. What we begin with is anonymous :—

> "This is Erinna's honeycomb, though small
> 'Tis of the Muses' sweets commingled all;
> Three hundred lines that match with Homer's lays:
> Such power this maid of nineteen years displays.
> Her mother's frown, the distaff and the loom
> Ordained, but for the Muses left some room.
> Sappho in lyrics o'er Erinna shone,
> But was in epic verse as much by her outdone."

Here is another by Antipater, translated by Merivale; a little altered :—

> "Few were thy words, Erinna, short thy lay,
> But thy short lay the Muse herself had given;
> Thus never shall thy memory decay,
> Nor night obscure thy fame, which lives in heav'n.

While we, the unnumbered bards of after-times,
   Sink in the melancholy grave unseen ;
Unhonoured reach Avernus' fabled climes,
   And leave no record that we once have been.

Sweet are the graceful swan's melodious lays,
   Though but an instant heard, and then they die ;
But the long chattering of discordant jays,
   The winds of April scatter through the sky."

Here is a catalogue of eight of the most distinguished lyric poets, to which the addition of Sappho would make a ninth ; but her sex, it is said, seems rather to recommend that she should be kept to make a tenth Muse. It is anonymous :—

"Pindar from Thebes gave forth a mighty shout :
Simonides melodious lays breathed out :
Stesichorus and Ibycus shone bright :
Alcman, Bacchylides, gave soft delight :
Persuasion dwelt on gay Anacreon's tongue :
Alcæus to Æolia nobly sung.
Sappho would make a ninth : but fitter she,
Among the Muses, a tenth Muse to be."

We may add here a somewhat similar enumeration, by another uncertain author, translated by Merivale. Here Sappho's name is included "to make up nine :"—

"O sacred voice of the Pierian choir,
   Immortal Pindar ! O enchanting air
Of sweet Bacchylides ! O rapturous lyre,
   Majestic graces, of the Lesbian fair !

Muse of Anacreon, the gay, the young !
Stesichorus, thy full Homeric stream !
Soft elegies by Cœa's poet sung !
Persuasive Ibycus, thy glowing theme !

> Sword of Alcæus, that, with tyrant's gore
> Gloriously painted, lift'st thy point so high!
> Ye tuneful nightingales that still deplore
> Your Alcman, prince of amorous poesy!
>   Oh yet impart some breath of heavenly fire
>   To him who venerates the Grecian lyre!"

A catalogue of female poets may here be given as a counterpart: it is by Antipater of Thessalonica:—

> "These god-tongued women were with song supplied
> From Helicon to steep Pieria's side:
> Prexilla, Myro, Anytè's grand voice—
> The female Homer;—Sappho, pride and choice
> Of Lesbian dames, whose locks have earned a name,
> Erinna, Telesilla known to fame.
> And thou, Corinna, whose bright numbers yield
> A vivid image of Athenè's shield.
> Soft-sounding Nossis, Myrtis of sweet song,
> Work-women all whose books will last full long.
> Nine Muses owe to Uranus their birth,
> And nine—an endless joy for man—to Earth."

Pindar is well entitled to one epigram all to himself, and it is here. It is by Antipater:—

> "As the war-trumpet drowns the fawn-bone flute,
> So, when your shell is heard, all else is mute.
> Not vainly did the swarm of brown bees drip
> Their wax-bound honey on your infant lip:
> Witness the hornèd god, aside who flings
> His pastoral reeds, and your high lyrics sings."

The dramatic poets come next in order.

On Æschylus.
By Dioscorides.

> "Thespis' invention, and the sylvan plays,
> And Bacchic games that gained the rustic's praise,

Æschylus raised aloft, and nobler made;
Not bringing carved and curious words to aid,
But like a torrent rushing down with force,
And stirring all things in its mighty course.
He changed the stage's forms: O voice sublime,
Fit for a demigod of ancient time."

On the Same.
By Diodorus.

"This tombstone tells, 'Here Æschylus is laid:'
By Gela's streams, from his own land afar:
Illustrious bard! what envious fate has made
Athenians ever with good men at war!"

On the Tomb of Sophocles.

By Simmias of Thebes: translation from the 'Spectator.'

"Wind, gentle evergreen, to form a shade
Around the tomb where Sophocles is laid.
Sweet ivy, lend thine aid, and intertwine
With blushing roses and the clustering vine.
Thus shall thy lasting leaves, with beauties hung,
Prove grateful emblems of the lays he sung."

These lines have been set to music in the form of a graceful catch or canon.

On Euripides.
Anonymous.

"Thou met'st, Euripides, a mournful fate!
When on thee wolf-dogs did their hunger sate!
The scene's sweet nightingale, the Athenians' pride!
Whose songs show grace with wisdom well allied,
At Pella thou hast found a tomb, that he
Who was the Muses' priest, should near the Muses be."

Euripides was said to have met his fate in a mysterious manner, being devoured at night by dogs, supposed to have been set on him by an enemy or rival.

An Inscription for his Cenotaph near Athens.

> "This tombstone is no monument of thee,
> But thou of it, Euripides, shall be :
> Thy glory clothes it, and men come to see."

On Aristophanes.
By Plato : translation by Merivale.

> "The Graces, seeking for a shrine,
> Whose glories ne'er should cease,
> Found, as they strayed, the soul divine
> Of Aristophanes."

This is good ; but it has, we think, at least one fault, in adding the epithet "divine." The original has it not : it contents itself with saying that the Graces found what they *did* find, and which it is inferred was just what they wanted. The following avoids that superfluity.

> "The Graces sought some holy ground,
> Whose site should ever please ;
> And in their search the soul they found
> Of Aristophanes."

The modest charm of "not too much" is one of the lessons which the best Greek compositions may teach us. The literal translation of the Greek is this :—

> "The Graces, seeking to possess some sacred enclosure which should never fail, found the soul of Aristophanes."

As Plato was a warm admirer of Aristophanes, it is

not improbable that he was the author of the beautiful and felicitous epigram referred to.

THE BOOKS OF ARISTOPHANES.
By Antipater of Thessalonica, translated by Dr Wellesley.

" The plays of Aristophanes! around that work divine
The Acharnian ivy's clust'ring wreaths in verdant glory
    twine.
What inspiration in the page! 'tis Bacchus' self!—What
    sounds
Of graceful poesy, which yet with dreaded wit abounds.
Genius of Comedy! how just! how true to all that's
    Greek!
Whate'er in satire or in jest thy personages speak."

ON MENANDER.
Anonymous.

" The bees themselves on thy lips honey dropped,
  Thence, where the Muses' flowers their zeal had cropped;
  The Graces, too, Menander, made thee know
  Of bright dramatic wit a happy flow.
  Thou'lt ever live; to Athens will be given
  A fame through thee to touch the clouds of heaven."

This survey of the poets may not unfitly be concluded by the epitaph on Leonidas of Tarentum, whether it be written by himself or by some one in his name. It discloses, apparently, a true account of the life of wandering and hardship that he had led. The translation is by Merivale :—

  " Far from Tarentum's native soil I lie,
    Far from the dear land of my infancy.
    'Tis dreadful to resign this mortal breath,
    But in a stranger clime 'tis worse than death!

Call it not life to pass a fevered age,
In ceaseless wanderings o'er the world's wide stage.
But me the Muse has ever loved, and giv'n
Sweet joys to counterpoise the curse of heav'n;
Nor lets my memory decay, but long
To distant times preserves my deathless song."

In what goes before, the poets exclusively have been dealt with; but a few epigrams are to be found upon historians and philosophers. The *jeu d'esprit* upon Herodotus which follows, is not a sufficient tribute to the merits of that delightful historian. It is by Leonidas of Alexandria, the translation by Mr de Teissier:

"The Muses to Herodotus one day
   Came, nine of them, and dined;
And in return, their host to pay,
   Left each a book behind."

It is well known that the history of Herodotus, in nine books, had the name of a Muse affixed to each.

On a Statue of Plutarch.
By Agathias: the translation by Dryden.
"Cheronean Plutarch, to thy deathless praise
Does' martial Rome this grateful statue raise:
Because both Greece and she thy fame have share'
(Their heroes written, and their lives compared);
But thou thyself couldst never write thy own;
Their lives have parallels, but thine has none."

To the Image of an Eagle near Plato's Tomb.
Anonymous.
"Eagle, why stand'st thou on that tomb, and why
Look'st thou aloft to yonder starry sky?"
"In me see Plato's soul, that heav'nward flies;
His earth-born corpse in Attic earth now lies."

It was a belief that the soul of a great and good man was carried to heaven by an eagle.

An Epitaph on Plato, by his Name of Aristocles.

"Excelling all in modesty and worth,
Godlike Aristocles here lies in earth;
If e'er 'twas given to reach high wisdom's praise,
'Twas given to him, nor did he envy raise."

The name of Plato was given to the philosopher from the great breadth either of his figure, or of his brow, or of his eloquence—it is not certain which.

On Plato and Esculapius.

"Plato and Esculapius both to Phœbus owed their birth,
Sent by the god of healing down, to succour men on earth.
To cure the body's maladies was one of these designed;
The other had the nobler charge of medicine for the mind."

This epigram alludes to the fiction that Plato, like Esculapius, was the son of Apollo, and not of a mortal father.

This is a shorter form of the same thought:—

"Asclepias once, and Plato, too, Phœbus to mortals gave,
That one the body, one the soul, from maladies might save."

On Epictetus.

By Leonidas.

"I, Epictetus, was a slave, who now lie buried here,
A cripple, and as Irus poor, and to the immortals dear."

On the Stoic Philosophy.
Anonymous.

"Ye Stoic sages, from your sacred leaves
The studious mind this highest truth receives,
That Virtue is the soul's ONE good, and she
Of men and nations the sole hope can be.
When fleshly pleasures others make their aim,
One Muse alone will her assent proclaim."

On Diogenes.
By Antiphilus.

"E'en brass grows old with time; but thy renown,
Diogenes, no age can e'er live down.
Thou only didst a self-sufficing way
And easy-going life to men display."

On the Study of Astronomy.
By Ptolemy: translation by P. Smyth.

"Though but the being of a day,
When I yon planet's course survey
This earth I then despise:
Near Jove's eternal throne I stand,
And quaff from an immortal hand
The nectar of the skies."

On Hypatia, the Female Astronomer.
Anonymous.

"When I behold thee—when I hear thy lore,—
Thy maiden presence humbly I adore.
I see in thee the Virgin of the sky,
The constellation shining there on high.
The heavens are still thy business and thy home,
To which thy lessons tend, from which they come;
Noble Hypatia! of high speech the flower,
The lustrous star of wise instruction's power."

What follows may connect these epigrams upon literature and philosophy with those that are immediately to come, as the subject of it will show.

On a Statue of Aristotle.
Anonymous.

" Here, from one mould, a statue we erect
To Aristotle—and to Intellect."

ARTISTIC.

We proceed now to those epigrams that illustrate the history and state of Art among the Greeks. These form a large proportion of the Anthology, and are more particularly to be found in the collection of Planudes.

The enormous destruction which in process of time has overtaken the works of ancient art, especially of ancient paintings, may prevent us from recognising in many epigrams allusions to statues and pictures which have now perished, where the epigrammatist may not have mentioned the artist's name, or stated explicitly the reference intended. Yet the industry of critics has latterly thrown a strong light on those subjects; and the discovery from time to time of ancient copies of lost works of art, and of miniature editions of them in gems or engraved stones, has facilitated greatly the proper understanding of this subject. We may notice one or two instances where an obscure hint so given in an epigram has been explained by an extant gem, and thus an additional interest conferred on both. Thus there is an anonymous epigram in Planudes which may be thus translated :—

> "The winged boy the winged thunder breaks :
> Thus Love o'er other fires precedence takes."

Many passages in ancient writers mention the existence of works of art representing Cupid holding a thunderbolt, and we read in Plutarch in particular that such a device was exhibited on Alcibiades' shield. But there is preserved an antique gem, of which an engraving is to be found in Spence's 'Polymetis,' Plate vii. fig. 3, where a winged Cupid is shown in the act of breaking a thunderbolt across his knee ; and it seems impossible to doubt that the writer of the epigram had seen or known of a work of art containing such a representation. Another epigram in Planudes runs thus—also anonymous :—

> "You there who blow that brand, your lamp to light,
> Light it at me : my soul is blazing quite."

This epigram, and another longer, to the same effect, seem to point to a sculptured Cupid blowing a torch into a blaze,—the same perhaps that Pliny mentions as a statue by Lycus, of a boy blowing into a flame a decaying fire.

The interest attached to these resemblances becomes, of course, all the greater when the question is as to works of art of a nobler kind. Indeed, the consideration of the connection between poetry and art, and of the mutual aid they have afforded each other, as well as the distinctions that separate them, lead to inquiries of greater importance and of a very attractive kind. Phidias is said to have declared that he derived his idea of the Olympian Jove from a few lines in Homer; while it is possible that Virgil drew, though with important modifications, his description of Laocoon and his sons from some work of art that he had seen, and which thus would have been the original of the group that we now possess. If, however, the artists copied from Virgil as the true source, this view is also full of interest, both as to the points of resemblance and those of diversity in the two representations.

In treating of the epigrams as illustrative of art, it is difficult to say in what order they should be dealt with. The periods at which the different epigrammatists lived is often so uncertain as to prevent the chronology of the authorship being taken as a guide. The best method seems to be to deal with the subjects according to their classes, and consequently to begin with the most dignified, those that relate to the gods.

Among the superlative achievements of ancient art must be reckoned the colossal statues of Minerva and Jupiter by Phidias, one of which stood in the Parthenon at Athens, and the other in the Temple of Jupiter at Olympia. In these works the Greek ideal of divinity was at last carried to its perfection. At first it would appear that the Greeks were satisfied with putting up images which partook more of the nature of symbols of the deity represented, than attempts at any supposed likeness; but by degrees it came to be established that the higher circle of gods should be exhibited as human forms, though transcendently more powerful and more beautiful than any human reality. The Olympian Jupiter of Phidias, which was his last work, attained the summit of this excellence. The material was that mixture of gold and ivory which got the name of Chryselephantine, and in which Phidias delighted to work. And the statue professed, as the artist himself declared, to be founded on the sublime passage in Homer, which describes the approving nod of the divinity, thus imposingly but not very accurately translated by Pope :—

> " He spoke, and awful bends his sable brows :
> Shakes his ambrosial curls, and gives the nod,
> The stamp of fate, and sanction of the god."

The work appears to have occupied Phidias, who was a slow and elaborate worker, for a period of from four to five years exclusively devoted to the task. A full and artistic account of the elaboration bestowed by him on his Minerva and Jupiter will be found in an article by Mr Story upon "Phidias and the Elgin Marbles" in 'Blackwood's Magazine' for December 1873.

Great as the reputation of Phidias must have been, there are not many allusions to him in the Anthologies. The principal of these, perhaps the only direct one, has reference apparently to the Olympian Jupiter, and is in these terms :—

> " Either Jove came to earth to show his form to thee,
> Phidias, or thou to heaven hast gone the god to see."

The rarity of such allusion may be more intelligible if we hold with high authorities, including Mr Story, that Phidias did not himself work in marble, so as to make his works more widely diffused.

Here is a short epigram by Julian upon an armed statue of Minerva in Athens. The allusion is to the contention said to have existed between her and Neptune for the sovereignty of Athens, in which Minerva was the conqueror. The epigrammatist remonstrates with the goddess for keeping on her armour after she had won the victory :—

" Why, Pallas, armed in Athens do you stand ?
Neptune has yielded ; spare the Athenian's land."

There seem to have been two statues—one of Minerva and one of Bacchus—placed near each other in some temple or public place, to which an epigrammatist addresses an inquiry of surprise as to the possible connection that thus placed them in proximity :—

" Say, Bacchus, why thus placed ? what can there be
In common held by Pallas and by thee ?
Her pleasure is in darts and battles: thine
In joyous feasts and draughts of rosy wine."
" Stranger, not rashly of the gods thus speak :
Our mutual likeness is not far to seek.
I, too, in battles glory—Indians know
In me, to ocean's edge, a conquering foe.
Mankind we both have bless'd ; the olive she
Has given, the vine's sweet clusters come from me.
Nor she, nor I, e'er caused a mother's pains:
I from Jove's thigh produced, she from his brains."

We have been led on somehow to pass over Juno, who

ought to have come after her husband. The most celebrated statue of her was that by Polycleitus at Argos, her favourite city, which was considered little if at all inferior to the works of Phidias. But to any image of Juno there is little reference in the Anthology. The most conspicuous notice is this, which apparently refers to the statue at Argos:—

> " The Argive Polycleitus, who alone
> Had sight of Juno, and that sight has shown,
> What of her beauty he could give, has given :
> Her unseen charms are kept for Jove in heaven.

As Jupiter was the great impersonation of majesty and power, so Juno was held to embody all the dignity of matronly excellence, being viewed in particular as the patroness of marriage, that institution on which civilised society is founded and family affection ingrafted. Perhaps the awe with which both Jupiter and Juno were regarded, and which was doubtless increased by the grandeur and beauty of their most celebrated statues, made of the most precious materials and of colossal magnitude, may have had some effect in keeping at least the lighter epigrammatists from trespassing on this ground. To some extent, also, the same feeling may have operated to preserve Minerva from being too familiarly dealt with ; though it will afterwards be seen that some of the poets did not scruple to introduce, with considerable levity, both Juno and Minerva in connection with their contest with Venus for the prize of beauty.

It need scarcely be said that the statues or likenesses

of Juno and Minerva were always presented in a draped form, though it is possible that the "white arms" of Juno, of which Homer speaks, may have sometimes been represented by sculptors. It seems not unlikely that until the time of Praxiteles the use of drapery was general with all or most of the goddesses. It is not easy otherwise to explain the point of the epigrams on the Cnidian Venus of that artist, which was exhibited undraped.

It is said that Praxiteles executed two statues of Venus,—one ordered by the Coans, entirely draped; another undraped, purchased by the Cnidians, and placed in a temple to the goddess as the bringer of prosperous navigation, in a position open to view from the shore and sea on all sides, in order probably that the sight of her image might give courage to the passing navigator, and might calm, or be thought to calm, the troubled deep within its range. It is to this Cnidian statue of Parian marble that the well-known epigram alludes which is ascribed to Plato—

"The Paphian Queen to Cnidos made repair
Across the tide, to see her image there:
Then looking up and round the prospect wide,
'Where did Praxiteles see me thus?' she cried."

This epigram has been expanded as well as abridged by other hands, but it is not worth while to give all these varieties, which turn a good deal upon mere conceits; as, for instance, that the chisel of the sculptor, being of steel, did the bidding of Mars by giving the marble all the beauty it could. We may give, however, an epigram of a lighter kind, borrowed from the first; and a third, of which the translation is partly borrowed from Merivale. The first runs thus:—

> "Said Venus when Venus in Cnidos she viewed:
> Fie! where did Praxiteles see me thus nude?"

Venus speaks:—

> "I'm certain, save Paris, Adonis, Anchises,
> No mortal e'er saw me when stripped of my clo'es:
> And if this be the case, then the question arises:
> Pray, how did Praxiteles see what he shows?"

Upon the same statue the following epigram also exists, by Evenus:—

> "That Cnidian work when they beheld,
> And saw how much its form excelled,
> Pallas and Juno both exclaimed,
> 'The Phrygian we unjustly blamed.'"

But another epigrammatist, anonymous, suggests with regard to the two statues of Pallas and Venus, at Athens and in Cnidos, that the spectator of each would for the time give the preference to that which was before his eyes. We give here Dr Wellesley's translation of the epigram referred to:—

> "When foam-sprung Venus' charms divine you view,
> You'll own the Phrygian herdsman's verdict true;
> But when the Athenian Pallas you survey,
> 'Oh, what a clown to pass her by!' you'll say."

There is a discussion in some of the old Greek authors as to the change of taste by which the Graces came ultimately to be represented in an undraped form, whereas the older artists all exhibited them as more or less clothed. Perhaps the explanation is that when Praxiteles, whose genius was certainly less exalted, and perhaps less unsensual, than that of his great predecessors, ventured to represent Venus herself as unclothed, the Graces, who were her handmaids, might be allowed to follow her example. That in older works of art they were usually draped is certain from several authorities, and is illustrated by an old epigram, said to be on a bath at Smyrna, of uncertain authorship, though attributed by some to Leontius. We give Dr Wellesley's translation :—

"While the Graces were taking a bath here one day,
Little Love with their goddess-ship's clothes made away
Then took to his heels, and here left them all bare,
Ashamed out of doors to be seen as they were."

In rivalry with the Cnidian Venus of Praxiteles may be ranked the equally celebrated Venus Anadyomene of Apelles. There are several epigrams on this subject, but of these two are conspicuous, one by Leonidas of Tarentum, and one by Antipater of Sidon. This is by Leonidas :—

"As Venus from her mother's bosom rose
(Her beauty with the murmuring sea-foam glows),
Apelles caught and fixed each heavenly charm;
No picture, but the life, sincere and warm.
See how those finger-tips her tresses wring!
See how those eyes a calm-like radiance fling!
That quince-formed breast reveals her in her prime,
Of love and soft desire the happy time.
Athenè and Jove's consort both avow—
'O Jove! we own that we are vanquished now.'"

This is by Antipater, borrowed, as he often does, from Leonidas. It chiefly deserves notice from the epithet Anadyomené ("emerging") being introduced:—

> "Venus, emerging from her parent sea,
>   Apelles' graphic skill does here portray:
> She wrings her hair, while round the bright drops flee,
>   And presses from her locks the foamy spray.
> Pallas and Juno now their claims give o'er,
> And say, 'In beauty we contend no more.'"

The reputed familiarity of Venus and Mars leads the epigrammatists sometimes to suppose her accoutred in his armour. The common books of gems show examples of this fancy; and from these or larger works of art on the subject the poets probably took the hint. This epigram is by Leonidas of Alexandria, the translation partly from Ogle (p. 12):—

> "These arms of Mars, why, Venus, do you wear?
>   Why the unwieldy weight for nothing bear?
> The god himself yields to your naked charms;
> To conquer men, what need of other arms?"

Conceits are to be found in the epigrams as to the power of Venus, if she were armed, to conquer still more easily those with whom she had contended when without armour; but Prior has well urged, what other poets had suggested, that the power of Venus lies truly in her *not* being armed.

Cupid has had almost enough of space bestowed upon him in a previous chapter, but we may give one or two more epigrams relating to him.

Several gems represent Cupid, or a plurality of

Cupids, making free with the armour or weapons of their betters. Several of these urchins are in one engraved stone seen combining to carry Hercules's club. Such images may have suggested the epigrams on the Loves appropriating the "attributes" of the gods in Olympus. This is a specimen; it is by Secundus :—

"See these all-plundering Loves! With boyish glee
On their stout backs they don heaven's panoply:
Bacchus' own drums and thyrse: Jove's thunderous fire:
The shield of Ares, and his dread attire:
Apollo's darts, Poseidon's three-toothed spear,
And the huge club Alcides used to rear.
What can men do, when Cupid conquers heaven,
And the gods' armour is to Venus given?"

Here is an epigram by Marcus Argentarius, obviously suggested by some engraving :—

"Love, the inevitable, here appears,
  Graved on a seal, reining the lion's might:
One hand the whip, and one the bridle bears,
  To urge and guide: here grace and force unite.
I fear the murderer: he who could subdue
This savage beast, must rule tame mortals too."

It is said that such a gem was at one time in the Orleans collection. In Spence's 'Polymetis' (Plate vii.) there is a representation of a Cupid riding on a lion and playing on the harp.

On Apollo there are not many direct epigrams, though he is celebrated in hymns and songs, which lie beyond our province. One epigram deserves to be inserted, as it refers to a celebrated bronze figure of him by Onatas. The epigram is a little obscure, and begins with a rather singular appellation applied to the god as an "ox-boy;" but the idea of ox-like dimensions seems to have presented to the Greek mind mainly the conception of full size, without any tinge of coarseness—as, for example, in the case of the "ox-eyed" Juno. The epigram is by Antipater of Thessalonica :—

> "Apollo here appears, a well-grown boy;
> Onatas' work in brass; a pride and joy
> To Jove and Leto : proof that not in vain
> Jove loved her; for by her we see again
> The power that in Jove's eyes and forehead reign.
> Nor should this work give pain to Juno's heart;
> Here Elithia crowns Onatas' art."

The epigrams referring to Diana are more numerous. We shall quote one or two of them. This is on a statue, by Diotimus :—

> "I am Diana, worthy of the name :
> My sire, none else than Jove, these looks proclaim.
> Confess, such maiden vigour here is found,
> All earth's too narrow for my hunting-ground."

This, which is anonymous, is supposed to refer to a picture :—

> "Where, Artemis, thy bow, thy quiver, too,
> Around thy neck, and the strong Cretan shoe;
> The gold that clasps thy robe, thy purple dress
> That shows thy knee in its full loveliness?"
> "Those for the chase I wear; but now not so:
> To meet men's offerings, it is thus I go."

Diana's Favour to Little Hounds.

"When little Calathine was brought to bed
Of pups, Diana well her labour sped.
Not only human mothers here find grace;
She aids her canine comrades of the chase."

But the most remarkable references to Apollo and Diana in the Anthology have relation to the story of Niobe, which will afterwards receive special consideration.

Bacchus has been already referred to as a subject of art, and we shall now give some more allusions to him.

Upon a Statue of Ariadne.
Anonymous.

"No mortal sculptor, Bacchus' self,
Thy lover, on this rocky shelf
Saw thee reclined, so heavenly fair,
And then for ever fixed thee there."

The following epigram by Evenus refers to a subject already noticed. Bland thus explains it:—
"The proportion of water with which the more moderate among the Grecian sages recommended that wine should be diluted was as three parts in four—a recommendation here ingeniously typified by linking Bacchus with three water-nymphs in the dance." The translation we give is by the younger Merivale, a little altered:—

"Water your wine to keep in moderation,
There's grief or madness in a strong potation.
For always it is Bacchus' highest pleasure
To move with Naiads three in mingled measure.

"'Tis there you'll find him famous company
For sports and loves and decent jollity;
But, when alone, avoid his fiery breath,
He breathes not love—but sleep, not far from death."

The second couplet would more nearly resemble the original thus:—

"For Bacchus still delights, where three Nymphs mingle,
To make a fourth, instead of keeping single."

Here is an epigram, said to be Plato's, upon one of Bacchus's attendants, a satyr, who, however, has taken the temperance pledge, and whose image as a water-bearer had been set up near a sleeping Cupid. The translation is from Bland, a little altered:—

"I from Dædalean hands my birth derive,
And so this solid stone was taught to live.
A Satyr, once enrolled in Bacchus' band,
But now a comrade of the Nymphs I stand.
In purple wine denied to revel more,
Sweet draughts of water from my urn I pour.
But, stranger, softly tread, lest any sound
Awake yon boy, in rosy slumbers bound."

Hermes or Mercury seems next to claim attention, and the variety of characters which this deity exhibited affords ample materials for reference to him. The most general idea that pervades his functions seems to be that of intercourse or communication. He was the patron of travellers, and presided over streets and highways. He was the messenger of the gods, and conveyed tidings from heaven to earth. He was the Soul-escorter from this world to the next; he facilitated communication among men by every means,—by language, by letters, and by merchandise. In these qualities lay that resemblance to the Teutonic deity, Odin or Woden, which led the Romans to consider that the Germans worshipped Mercury. A trace of that supposed connection is still to be seen in the names given by the English and French to the middle day of the week.

One mode of communication or interchange practised and protected by Mercury was more objectionable than others. He was the god of thieves, and an adept in that irregular means of transferring property. He would no doubt have been pleased with the euphemism of Shakespeare's Pistol—"*Convey*, the wise it call." He patronised other arts, such as music and gymnastics; and these, too, were connected with social intercourse. His humblest office, probably, was that of a milestone, in which form he frequently figured. This epigram is an example,—it is anonymous:—

> " To Mercury some travellers set up Me,
> A heap of stones : small honour *that* could be.
> So, as a like return, he bids me tell—
> 'Tis hence seven stadia to the she-goat's well."

The next gives him a better position and more beneficent duties :—

> " Me, Hermes, near this breezy garden see !
> On the highway and by the grey sea-shore ;
> To wearied men a resting-place to be,
> While cooling waters from the fresh founts pour."

ON A STATUE OF HERMES, BY SCOPAS.
Anonymous.

"Good friend, don't think that here you see
A common Mercury in me:
A nobler deity I stand;
The workmanship of Scopas' hand."

As Mercury was often set up over fields and gardens to protect them from pillage, this was a delicate position for one of his principles, which is pretty well brought out in this epigram:—

THE PASSENGER AND MERCURY.

"This cabbage, Hermes, may I clutch?"
"No, passenger, you must not touch."
"So stingy?" "No, but law commands
From others' goods to keep your hands."
"Ah, well! but I can scarce believe
'Tis Hermes tells me—not to thieve."

Our next epigram shows the same god as suffering from his own pupils and principles. It is by Lucillius, the translation by Cowper:—

"When Aulus, the nocturnal thief, made prize
Of Hermes, swift-winged envoy of the skies,—
Hermes, Arcadia's king, the thief divine,
Who when an infant stole Apollo's kine,
And whom, as arbiter and overseer
Of our gymnastic sports, we planted here;—
'Hermes,' he cried, 'you meet no new disaster;
Ofttimes the pupil goes beyond his master.'"

UPON THE STATUE OF A BEARDLESS MERCURY SET UP NEAR A BOYS' RACE-COURSE.

"Who set thee, beardless Hermes, here, this starting-post
to grace?"

"Hermogenes." "Of whom the son?" "Of Daimoneus."
"What place?"
"Of Antioch." "Why this honour done?" "My needful
help he found
In running." "Where?" "On Isthmian both and on
Nemèan ground."
"He ran?" "And came in first." "O'er whom?" "O'er
boys in number *nine;*
And then he flew as if his feet had wings as good as mine."

It would be tedious to go over all the deities to
whom the epigrams may refer, or to the statues or paintings representing them. Enough has perhaps been
said to awaken interest in the subject; and it will be
remembered that the object of these observations is not
to give a history of art or a manual of mythology, but
to show by striking examples the mutual connection of
art and this form of poetry. We may dismiss the
chapter of the gods by a reference to two interesting
subjects. Mention has already been made of Venus as
the promoter of prosperous navigation. In that character she had other names, or had the aid of assistant
goddesses that did her bidding. An epigram of
Addæus expressly refers to and describes an engraved
stone by Tryphon, representing Galenè, the goddess of
calm, one of those propitious deities, and it is believed
that extant gems exhibit the same subject:—

"An Indian beryl, Tryphon won me o'er
To spread into a calm from shore to shore.
Galenè's name and form he bade me bear,
And his soft hands let flow my lengthening hair.
See how my kisses soothe the watery deep,
And how my bosom lulls the waves to sleep!

>   Did not the envious stone my will confine,
>   You'd see me quickly floating on the brine."

One of the most remarkable of the minor Greek deities was Nemesis, who seems scarcely to be represented by any Roman equivalent, unless we call her Divine Vengeance. In superstitious minds among the Greeks the idea appears to have existed that the gods were envious of the good fortune of men, and on that account visited them with affliction; and we often find the feeling of envy ascribed to Death or Hades in carrying off the young and lovely. But Nemesis, we would fain think, had a higher origin and position in the estimation of pious and reverential men. It was her function to prescribe moderation in all things, and to check all arrogance or presumption, and with that view to remind men of the mutability of events, and the instability of mortal possessions. Nemesis is not merely the avenger of actual crime, but the represser of inordinate thoughts and pretensions of all kinds. Such an influence is to be found in all religious systems, and is experienced by all reflecting men. The story of Polycrates's ring presents a pagan illustration of it. The simple and amiable wife of Marmontel had something of that feeling: "'Nous sommes trop heureux,' me disait ma femme; 'il nous arrivera quelque malheur.'"

Two epigrams may here be given describing Nemesis by her usual accompaniments—a measuring rule, or her own fore-arm raised, and a bridle.

This is by an anonymous writer:—

>   " Nemesis checks, with cubit-rule and bridle,
>   Immoderate deeds, and boastings rash and idle."

This also is anonymous; it may be thus translated :—

"I, Nemesis, this cubit hold; you ask the reason why?
'Let nothing in excess be done;' with this let all comply."

Mr King, in his 'Handbook' (p. 367), gives us the engraving of a gem representing the Twin Nemeses, patronesses of Smyrna. "One holds a bridle, the other a measuring wand, and raises at the same time her fore-arm or cubitus, thus typifying both self-restraint and moderation." In another of Mr King's books (his illustrations of Mr Munro's 'Horace'), a different gem is exhibited, in which Nemesis is represented without the bridle, but merely with her fore-arm uplifted, and with an ash-branch in her hand, while her brow is bent downwards under the bosom of her robe.

It was at one time supposed that Phidias was either the sculptor or had superintended the formation of a celebrated statue of Nemesis placed in the temple of that deity at Rhamnus, and connected in some way with the battle of Marathon. This statue has been the subject of a good deal of apocryphal or doubtful tradition, referred to by Mr King in the 'Illustrated Horace.' It was said that the Persians, when they invaded Greece before the battle of Marathon, had brought from the island of Paros, which they passed in their voyage, a block of marble for a trophy to be erected in Greece in honour of their anticipated victories; but that when they were defeated at Marathon, the Greeks had seized the stone, and converted it into a statue of Nemesis, to be erected in her temple at Rhamnus, which is near Marathon. The following epigram is extant in commemoration of this supposed incident,—a tempting subject for an epigrammatist:—

> "ME Persians brought a trophy here to be
> Of victory; now a Nemesis they see.
> Nay, both; to Greece a trophy I shall stand,
> To Persia, proof of Nemesis' high hand."

It is now suspected, however, that this tradition is what Mr Story calls it, a pure "myth;" and this belief would be confirmed if we suppose that the Rhamnusian statue in the Elgin room of the British Museum was this Nemesis; for it seems to be certain, "from the recent examination of intelligent judges, that this celebrated statue was not of Parian but of Pentelic marble," which is quite distinguishable from Parian. Another question remains,—Whether the Rhamnusian statue was by Phidias or not? as to which the preponderance of evidence seems to be that it was the work of his pupil and friend Agoracritos, whose name was put as the maker of it on the branch of an ash-tree held in the hand of the goddess. A story was also told of Agoracritos having first made a statue of Venus, and that having failed to obtain the prize for it, the preference being given to another sculptor, he was so indignant that, after making certain alterations, he sold it to the people of Rhamnus as a Nemesis—which is also probably a myth.

On the supposition of the intended Persian trophy being converted by the Greeks into a Nemesis, Dr Wellesley, in his Polyglot Anthology, refers to a parallel incident in the conversion of a stone of Buonaparte's column, intended to commemorate the successful invasion of England, being afterwards used to record the restoration of the Bourbons,—and on that subject he gives us the following epigram :—

> "Frenchmen, who brought this marble block to stand
> A trophy of the invasion of yon land,
> Behold! it marks a Bourbon's restoration,
> And tells that you are the invaded nation."

Something of the same sort happened to a French pillar at Coblentz which the Russians adopted.

The only result that we feel assured of in connection with the Nemesis at Rhamnus seems to be, that soon after the battle of Marathon, and probably out of the Persian spoils, which were of great value, a new statue of that goddess was erected at her favourite seat in Greece, where it long remained.

Nemesis seems to have been treated as a real goddess; but there were impersonations of abstract powers which scarcely attained that rank, yet were made the subject of artistic representation, and are referred to in the epigrams accordingly. One of the most striking of these was Opportunity, of which Lysippus made a very remarkable statue, the subject of a clever epigram by Posidippus, of which a translation shall now be given :

> "The sculptor whence?" "From Sicyon." "Who?"
>   "Lysippus is his name."
> "And you?" "I'm Opportunity, that all things rule and
>   tame."
> "On tiptoe why?" "I always run." "Why winglets
>   on your feet—
> And double too?" "Before the wind I fly with progress
>   fleet."

"Why is a razor in your hand?" "To teach men this to know,
That sharper than a razor's edge the times for action grow."
"Why this lock on your forehead?" "That you all may seize me there."
"And why then is your occiput so very bald and bare?"
"That none who once have let me pass may ever have the power
To pull me back, and bring again the once-neglected hour."
"Why did the artist fashion you?" "For your instruction, friend,
And placed me in this vestibule these lessons to commend."

This epigram was translated by Ausonius, who, from error or design, stated the artist of the statue to be Phidias,—an error which leads one to suspect that he was not a very good judge of art, or well acquainted with its history.

We proceed next to those epigrams that relate to demigods and heroes, with their images. Of these Hercules may be considered the first and greatest. The myths of this deity present some singular features. The radical idea impersonates the perfection of bodily strength, and thus completes the cycle of artistic development in the human form, which had already comprised Jupiter as the emblem of majesty, Apollo of manly beauty, Hermes of activity and agility. But the bulky strength of Hercules is at the same time accompanied by a less perfect intellectual organisation. Some of the philosophical teachers, and in particular Prodicus, in his well-known and very beautiful apologue, represents him as deliberately making his choice, at his entry upon active life, between the rival invitations of Virtue and Pleasure; but the popular notion encroaches upon this ideal, and shows him always, indeed, as a redresser of wrongs and an abater of nuisances, but also as not unfrequently seduced into some of the vices to which corporeal strength is occasionally subject, such as gluttony and drunkenness, and facility under female influence. No character is oftener chosen as the subject both of artistic and of epigrammatic representation than this hero in the various phases of his development. His first achievement in strangling the serpents sent against him by Juno is seen on several gems, of which two will be found in Spence's book. The following epigram on that subject is by an unknown author:—

"Crush, Hercules, with all that infant strength,
Those dragon folds, those throats of giant length:
Strive to appease even now the fury wild
Of Juno; learn to labour, yet a child.
No brazen cup or caldron is the prize,
But the bright road that leads to yonder skies."

Spence's book gives well-known engravings forming a complete series of Hercules's twelve labours, and there are several epigrams that enumerate them. We insert one by Philippus as a specimen:—

"The Nemean monster, and the Hydra dire
I quelled: the Bull, the Boar, I saw expire
Under my hands; I seized the queenly Zone,
And Diomede's fierce steeds I made my own.
I plucked the golden Apples: Geryon slew:
And what I could achieve Augèas knew:
The Hind I caught: the vile Birds ceased their flight:
Cerberus I upwards dragged; and gained Olympus' height."

This special epigram on his combat with the lion, by Damagetus, is believed to refer to a statue of Hercules while engaged in that struggle, which stood in Rome in the time of Ovid, and which is thought to have been afterwards removed to Byzantium, and much admired there :—

> "The Nemean Lion and the Argive guest,—
> Of wild beasts and of demigods the best,—
> Engage in combat, each with scowling eye,
> To solve the issue, who shall live or die.
> Jove, let the Argive man the victor be,
> That Nemea safe again to traverse we may see."

Another special epigram on his killing the Mænalian Hind, by an anonymous author, describes accurately the attitude depicted in all the artistic representations of that achievement :—

> "How shall my gazing eyes and thoughtful mind
> Enough admire the Hero and the Hind?
> On the beast's loins his knee is firmly set,
> While on her branching horns his hands have met.
> She, breathing heavily with lips apart,
> Shows by her tongue the pressure at her heart.
> Rejoice, Alcides; we in her behold
> Not the horns only, but the whole of gold."

On a Statue of Hercules and Antæus.
The translation by Hay.

> "Who hath impressed on brass that mournful air
> Of one who struggles 'gainst Alcides' might?
> Instinct with life, there force and fierce despair
> Fill us with mingled pity and affright.
> Under Alcides' grasp Antæus see,
> Writhing and groaning in his agony."

We have here rather a different picture of the youth who had made the path of virtue his choice :—

HERCULES IN A STATE OF EBRIETY.

" This, the all-conquering hero, brave and strong,
For his twelve labours famed in poets' song,
Heavy with drink, now staggers in his gait,
Subdued by Bacchus to this helpless state."

We formerly had an epigram assimilating the rather incongruous characters of Minerva and Bacchus. Here there is one of the same nature, suggested by the associated statues of Bacchus and Hercules :—

" Both Thebans, warriors both, and sons of Jove :
That Thyrsus, and this Club, our terror move :
Of like extent their toils : their garbs akin,
Clad in the faun's or in the lion's skin ;
One loves the cymbals, one the rattle's din.
Juno to both was hostile, but each came
From earth to heaven by paths that led through flame."

Bacchus used the cymbals in his Indian conquests; Hercules the rattle in one of his labours, that of frightening away the Stymphalides : Bacchus was deified through the fate of his mother Semelè ; Hercules ascended to heaven from his great funeral pyre.

In the next epigram we have Hercules contrasted with another god, Mercury, in their character of guardians of the shepherds' flocks :—

" Ye shepherds, Hermes can be won with ease ;
A little milk or honey's sure to please :
Not so Alcides ; he demands a ram,
All to himself, or at the least a lamb.
What though he checks the wolves ? 'tis nought to me
Which of them eats my sheep, the wolf or he."

There is a paraphrase by Prior of the latter part of this epigram, in which the shepherd positively refuses to pay "black-mail" to Hercules for protecting him against robbery:—

> "When hungry wolves had trespass'd on the fold,
> And the robbed shepherd his sad story told;
> 'Call in Alcides,' said a crafty priest;
> 'Give him one half, and he'll secure the rest.'
> 'No!' said the shepherd; 'if the Fates decree,
> By ravaging my flock to ruin me,
> To their commands I willingly resign,—
> Power is their character, and patience mine;
> Though, troth, to me there seems but little odds
> Who prove the greatest robbers, wolves or gods!'"

Hercules had always a character for voracity, and no doubt needed large supplies of food to support that bulky frame, such as the Farnese Hercules may still show us. In another epigram Hermes complains of not getting his fair share of the offerings made jointly to him and Hercules, as associated together in watching the boundaries between two estates or territories:—

> "Ye friends who pass this way, whether you come
> From town or country, whichsoe'er your home,
> Here we two gods, to guard these marches set,
> I Mercury, he Hercules, are met.
> Both willing to oblige: but our reward
> Is far from equal for thus mounting guard.
> My pears, my figs, I see him still devour:
> He does not leave me even the stale or sour.
> I hate this partnership! what gifts you bear,
> Bring them in portions, giving each his share;
> And say, 'Here, Hercules,' and 'Hermes, here,'
> And thus our feud at last may disappear."

Hercules was a favourite subject of representation with the eminent sculptor Lysippus, who among other honours had the monopoly of making statues of Alexander the Great. A statue of Hercules by Lysippus exhibited him in a depressed state, apparently from love, and to this the following epigram by Geminus is considered to allude :—

ON A BRONZE STATUE, BY LYSIPPUS, OF HERCULES DEPRESSED.

"Where, Hercules, thy club, thy lion's skin,
Thy bow, thy quiver, with its darts within
Where thy proud look ? why did Lysippus' art
Such pain, such sadness, to the bronze impart ?
Stripped of thine arms thou griev'st : who used thee so?
The wingèd Love, the one resistless foe."

Theseus is another hero of illustrious name. He is said to have followed in Hercules's footsteps, though he was not deified so authentically as his prototype. There is an epigram upon a statue said to have represented his combat with the Marathonian bull. But there have been found several gems, and a remarkable mosaic, representing undoubtedly the combat of Theseus with the Minotaur ; and it is not impossible that the epigram in question relates to that subject. It is anonymous :—

"A miracle of art ! this deadly fight :
The man bears down the bull with matchless might.
With knee upon his foe his hands he lays,
One on the nostrils, one the horn to raise :

> He twists the neck-joints with a fatal clasp,
> And back the monster falls with struggling gasp.
> Who sees the skilful brass, would think he viewed
> The beast's quick breath, the man with sweat bedewed."

Salmoneus was not a hero, but he affected to be a god. A picture of him was painted by Polygnotus, on which there is this epigram by Geminus :—

> Me Polygnotus' hand produced : with Jove
> In rival thunderings, I, Salmoneus, strove :
> Though I'm in Hades now, his thunders seek
> My likeness, which no boasting words can speak.
> Spare, Jove, your bolts : give o'er the inglorious strife :
> War not with images, devoid of life."

One sees here an example of the confusion of ideas which the epigrammatist, perhaps wilfully, introduces, as if to puzzle his reader. The picture showed Jupiter directing his thunder against Salmoneus. But if Salmoneus was but a dead image, so was Jupiter himself.

The story of Niobe forms a frequent subject of epigrams, and may be considered in this place. It is hopeless to attempt any strict order of chronology as to personages and events that may possibly be altogether fabulous.

The father of Niobe was Tantalus, who was honoured by the friendship and hospitality of Jupiter, but unfortunately got into disgrace by repeating some confidential communication which had been made to him at Jupiter's table. This no doubt was very wrong, but the punishment inflicted was rather severe. He was placed in Tartarus, and suffered perpetual hunger and thirst; while a huge stone, impending over him, threatened constantly to destroy him. The following epigram, by Ælius Gallus, relates to his punishment. The version is taken chiefly from that of Hay:—

ON A TANTALUS SCULPTURED ON A DRINKING-CUP.

"See how the guest of gods, who often quaffed
    The nectar's purple juice, now longs to sip
A drop of water—while the envious draught
    Shrinks downward, far away from that parched lip
In silence drink,' this sculpture says, 'and know
A froward tongue brought such excess of woe.'"

Niobe, like her father, became an object of divine resentment for a similar fault, incontinence of tongue. Becoming the mother, as some say, of fourteen children, she could not refrain from boasting of her preeminence in fertility over Latona, the mother of only a pair, Apollo and Diana. These deities avenged the insult by destroying all Niobe's children and turning herself to stone, or allowing her grief to have that effect. Sculptors were fond of representing her fate, and in particular a group of statues was produced, which was ultimately brought to Rome, and of which it was doubted whether Praxiteles or Scopas was the artist. It seems now to be considered certain that Scopas has the merit. In later times this group, or ancient duplicates of it, were found in Italy, and in 1770 the statues so found were removed to Florence, where they are known as the Niobids, and are deservedly admired as of first-rate excellence. Here is one of the epigrams upon Niobe, by Antipater of Sidon:—

"Tantalus' daughter this : once proud to show
  Her fourteen children—now, oh sight of woe !
A monumental victim here she stands
  Of Phœbus and Diana's vengeful hands.
He all the sons—she all the daughters slew—
  At once twice Seven were stripped of life by Two.
The mother of so many thus bereft,
  Had not even one to soothe her sorrows left.
Not, as is wont, did children deck her tomb ;
  To bury *them* was here the parent's doom.
Sins of the tongue on her, as on her sire,
  Brought down in varying forms celestial ire :
She, turned to stone ; he, filled with fear and dread,
  With that huge rock impending o'er his head."

The next that we give presents the story in a more dramatic form, and is by Meleager, translated by Hay. A messenger speaks:—

"Daughter of Tantalus, lorn Niobe,
  Sad are the tidings which I bear to thee,
Words fraught with woe : ay, now unbind thy hair,
  The streaming signal of thy wild despair :
For Phœbus' darts grief-painted reek with gore,
  Alas ! alas !—thy sons are now no more.
But what is this—what means this oozing flood !
  Her daughters, too, are weltering in their blood.
One clasps a mother's knees, one clings around
  Her neck, and one lies prostrate on the ground :
One seeks her breast : one eyes the coming woe,
  And shudders : one is trembling, crouching low :
The seventh is breathing out her latest sigh,
  And life-in-death is flickering in that eye.
She—the woe-stricken mother—left alone,
  Erst full of words—is now mute-stricken stone."

A part of the tradition seems to have been that Niobe, thus transformed, was carried off in a whirlwind and fixed on the top of a mountain in Phrygia, which Pausanias says he visited, when he saw in the mountain, not near at hand but at a certain distance, the likeness of a woman weeping. Ovid embodies this part of the story in the account of her in his 'Metamorphoses:'—

> " Borne on the whirlwind to her native land,
> See on the mountain-top the statue stand.
> There ever fixed, still weeping she appears,
> And from the marble mass even now distil the tears."

A playful epigram on the subject of Niobe proceeds on the mistaken idea that Praxiteles was the artist by whom her statue was made. It runs thus:—

> " Me the gods turned to stone, but turned in vain;
> Praxiteles has made me live again."

The story of Medea is another frequent and favourite subject of art, to which several epigrams refer in a manner full of interest.

Among the painters of antiquity, few have a greater name than Timomachus, who is mentioned with high praise by the best ancient writers upon art. Two of his pictures were bought by Julius Cæsar at the price of eighty talents, equal to about £20,000, and placed by him in the temple which he dedicated to Venus Genetrix, as the ancestress of the Julian race. These two works which came thus to be publicly accessible at Rome, are the subjects of several epigrams. One of these pictures, representing Medea preparing to destroy her children, out of resentment against Jason her husband, is expressly dealt with by different epigrammatists, who notice its most distinguishing excellence in representing in Medea's features the conflict between parental love and conjugal jealousy and rage. It is believed that Antiphilus, who flourished in the first century of our era, led the way in putting this encomium into a poetical shape, but he was followed by others. The title is—

Upon a Likeness of Medea at Rome.

"Timomachus, when his skilled hand designed
 To paint Medea's much distracted mind,
Chose a great task, the double power to prove
 Of jealous hatred and maternal love.
One passion asked a look to anger bent,
And one as strongly to compassion leant.
Both he achieved: the picture tells the truth;
Tears mix with threats, and rage combines with ruth.
Delay was here most wise: the deed thus planned
Befits Medea's not the artist's hand."

This is a shorter form of the same idea, by an anonymous author:—

"Timomachus has in Medea's face
 Her hate and mother's love at once portrayed:
Here jealous rage, affection there we trace;
 Thus seems her children's fate a while delayed.
She longs to wield, she fears to use, the glaive—
Wishing at once to slay them and to save."

Lessing, in his Laocoon, that admirable exposition of the differing objects and limits of poetry and the fine arts, has commented on the judgment shown by Timomachus in choosing as the time of his representation, not the actual murder of Medea's children, but the moment before it, when we anticipate the result, but are saved the repulsive pain of witnessing it. Another Greek epigram on the same subject has expressed the very principle contended for by Lessing—namely, that the mimetic arts of painting and sculpture ought not to perpetuate by their unchanging representations the extreme limits of what is horrible or shocking. The lines are :-

> " Wisely the artist has the end concealed,
> Lest admiration should to horror yield."

Lessing says that the praise thus deservedly earned by Timomachus contrasts with the censure directed in an epigram by Philippus against another artist, who had represented Medea in the full height of her frenzy, without any mixture of a milder emotion. We are not sure upon what authority this is stated ; but here is a translation of the epigram, though the text is not without difficulties, and seems partially corrupt :—

> "Who breathed, thou lawless Colchian, such fierce ire
> Into thy likeness, such barbarian fire ?
> Thy children's blood dost thou yet thirst to spill ?
> Glaucè again for a new Jason kill ?
> Hence, cursed murderess, whose relentless heart
> Dares to infect with hate the painter's art !"

The Ajax of the same painter was also much admired, as exhibiting a similar feeling of propriety and soundness of judgment. The subject is the insanity of

Ajax, following upon the decision of the Greeks which awarded the arms of Achilles not to him but to Ulysses. The contest is admirably narrated in the 13th Book of Ovid's 'Metamorphoses,' of which Dryden has given an excellent version.

The effect of the judgment on Ajax is thus described by Ovid:—

> "He who could often and alone withstand
> The foe, the fire, and Jove's own partial hand,
> Now cannot his unmastered grief sustain,
> But yields to rage, to madness, and disdain.
> Then snatching out his falchion, 'Thou,' said he,
> 'Art mine; Ulysses lays no claim to thee.
> Oh, often-tried and ever-trusty sword,
> Now do thy last kind office to thy lord.
> 'Tis Ajax who requests thy aid, to show
> None but himself himself could overthrow."

But Ovid does not mention the intermediate effects of Ajax's insanity, during which he is said to have attacked and slaughtered the sheep and oxen in the fields, in the belief that they were the Greek judges who had denied him his rights. In Timomachus's picture, however, as Lessing observes, "he was not represented in the height of his paroxysm, slaughtering the rams and the he-goats, which he mistakes for his enemies; but in the state of exhaustion which succeeded to these feats, revisited by reason, and meditating self-destruction. And this in strict meaning is the "Distracted Ajax" of the tragedy: not that he is so now, but because we see his distraction expounded by its effects, and the enormity of it measured by the acuteness of his shame.

Several poems in the Anthology have reference to Ajax, and some of them undoubtedly to this picture by Timomachus. This is an anonymous one:—

"Ajax, Timomachus may better claim
 To be your sire than he who bears the name :*
 Art has assumed the place of Nature's power.
 The painter saw you in your frenzied hour,
 And his hand caught the madness. Grief appears,
 Mixed in each varied form of pain and tears."

This that follows, by Leonidas, not of Tarentum, is understood by some critics—with great probability, we think—to represent "the words that Ajax would have spoken when about to destroy himself:"—

"I now, whom Mars was still afraid to slay,
 Struck by an inward foe, here waste away.
 Come, sword, my bosom pierce! drive hence afar,
 With manly force, disease as well as war."

Gravelle,† in his 'Ancient Gems,' gives a stone representing the suicide of a hero, which he considers to apply to Ajax.

Ajax seems to have been a favourite with the epigrammatists as well as with the artists, as there are several epigrams upon his defeat in his contest for the armour of Achilles, and upon his consequent suicide. We give some examples.

This is by Asclepiades, perhaps referring to some work of art :—

---

* Telamon.   † Gravelle, ii. 60.

"I, Valour, wretched maid, sit here forlorn
By Ajax' tomb, my locks for sorrow shorn:
Grieved at my heart, among the Greeks to see
Crafty and base Deceit preferred to me."

The next, by an uncertain author, refers to his suicide, and may have been borrowed from Ovid:—

"Of Telamonian Ajax this the tomb:
From his own hand and sword he met his doom·
For Fate, though willing, found no other way
A hero so invincible to slay."

Here is a singular epigram on Ajax, of which the text seems not very pure, and the allusions require explanation:—

"Beside brave Ajax' tomb a Phrygian stood,
And mocked the chief with ribald words and rude.
'Ajax no more stood firm,' the scoffer said:
'He did stand firm,' cried out the indignant dead;
Whereat, in fear, the living Phrygian fled."

The tomb of Ajax, on the Trojan plain, was obnoxious to the natives, who retained the tradition of his having destroyed their cattle in his madness. The peasants used to utter maledictions against him over his grave; but the story was told that on one occasion a shout came from the earth which put to flight his calumniators. In the epigram above quoted, the reproach urged against Ajax is taken from a line in the 15th Book of Homer, where Ajax is represented as retiring for a moment before Hector's attack on the Grecian ships; but he rallied immediately, and achieved prodigies of valour.

The incidents of the Trojan War were frequent

subjects of artistic representation. With consummate art, Virgil, in the Æneid, leads his shipwrecked hero to a temple in Carthage, where already the tale of Troy had been, in full detail, sculptured or painted on the wall. If our readers will turn to the volume of this series which contains Virgil, p. 51, they will find an animated description of the scene; and the whole passage may be read with pleasure in Dryden's translation, though it may be doubted if there was not a certain degree of anachronism in supposing so early an advance in art.

Among the most celebrated of actual pictures on Homeric subjects are those which the painter Polygnotus executed for the Lesche or Conversation-room at Delphi, as an offering by the Cnidians to Apollo. One of these was the "Taking of Troy," to which was attached an epigram ascribed to Simonides. The translation is somewhat too paraphrastic :—

" This picture, traced by Polygnotus' hand,—
(Aglaophon's son, and born on Thasos' strand),—
To tell its wondrous tale has here been placed,
And show the citadel of Troy laid waste."

There still survive, in the form of gems or engraved stones, miniature representations of Trojan events, of which the larger pictures or sculptures may have supplied themes for descriptive epigrams. The works treating of ancient gems contain much interesting information on this subject. In particular, Mr King's beautiful books on the Glyptic Art show us a full series of gems still preserved on classical mythology, on the epic cycles, and on Trojan tradition, which may readily be connected with many epigrams. Spence's 'Polymetis,' already referred to, though an old-fashioned book, will also be of use. Some of the epigrams alluded to have already been given, and we shall now notice a few others.

One of the gems represents Æneas issuing from the gates of Troy with Anchises upon his shoulder, and leading the boy Ascanius in his hand. The following epigram relates to that subject, and perhaps has reference to the work of art from which the gem was taken :—

"From burning Troy, from ranks of hostile spears,
 Æneas laden with his sire appears ;
 A holy burden for a pious son !
'Spare him, ye Greeks,' he cries ; 'no glory's won
 O'er an old man in battle : but to me,
 Bearing him safe, how great the gain will be !'"

The story of Philoctetes, too, belongs to the cycle of the Trojan War, and was also a common subject of art.

Here are two epigrams upon him : the first upon a picture by Parrhasius, who used to boast that he saw in sleep or in his mind's eye everything that he painted ; the other is upon a piece of sculpture :—

"Trachinian Philoctetes, wretched wight !
 Parrhasius drew, such as he met his sight.
'Twixt his parched eyelids lurks the languid tear,
 And all his wasting toil is pictured here.
Thou best of artists, great thy skill, but oh !
 'Twas time to free him from this tearful woe !"

"Worse than the Greeks, a new Ulysses, he,
Who sculptured thus my wound and agony.
This rock, these rags are sad—the sore, the pain;
But now in brass, my misery must remain."

The following epigram relates obviously to a picture of Capaneus at the siege of Thebes, an event earlier than the Trojan War. Capaneus was struck by lightning from Jupiter for his presumption, and this gives the epigrammatist his hint. The picture was by Polygnotus:—

"Had Capaneus at Thebes such rage displayed,
When, its high towers to scale, his feet essayed,
The city had been stormed in fate's despite,
For even Jove's bolts had feared with him to fight."

Though somewhat out of place in the order of time to which the works of art referred to may seem to belong, we shall here insert two epigrams connected with the well-known story of Arion, of whom there was erected a statue at Corinth, representing also the dolphin which brought him safe to land:—

"When sweet Arion, Cycles' son, implored the aid of Heaven,
To bear him from Sicilian seas was this Conveyance given."

"This image of Arion here—great Periander placed,
And of the Dolphin who gave aid with such effectual haste,
Saving from death the sinking bard: Arion's fable shows,
From men we oft destruction meet, from fish salvation flows."

Leaving now gods and heroes, and fabulous persons

and events, we may proceed to those works of art, or rather to those epigrams upon such works, which deal with realities. One of the most distinguished of the second class of artists was Myro, or Myron, who, though he aspired occasionally to represent deities or heroes, was yet more at home on humbler subjects. A proof of this is perhaps to be found in the importance which was attached to his celebrated statue of a heifer, on which an interminable quantity of epigrams was written. We shall not trouble our readers with many of these, for it must be acknowledged that they constitute a very idle assemblage of laborious trifles. One of them we shall give as a specimen, from which the character of the others may be inferred. It is by Antipater:—

"Methinks this heifer is about to low:
So, not Prometheus only, Myron, thou,
Like him, with life canst lifeless things endow."

Myro made a statue of Bacchus also, to which the following epigram refers:—

"Bacchus, once more you from the fire come forth;
'Tis Myron now who gave this second birth."

Besides these subjects, Myron particularly excelled in athletic figures. The victors in the public games were frequent subjects of art, especially of sculpture, and are so referred to in many epigrams, whether actual or descriptive. Here is one by Simonides, which it is probable was actually inscribed on a statue of Milo, the celebrated athlete:—

> "This, Milo's image! wondrous fair to see,
> Of a form wondrous fair! at Pisa he
> Victor seven times, to none e'er bowed the knee."

The speed of Ladas as a runner was much extolled by ancient writers; there were two of the name, the more celebrated of the two being an Argive, who was hyperbolically said to run with such velocity and lightness that he left no traces of his steps in the dust over which he passed. He is referred to in several epigrams more or less seriously. This is one by an unknown writer:—

> "If Ladas ran or flew, in that last race,
> Who knows? 'twas such a *demon* of a pace."

To which another couplet was added, to this effect:—

> "Scarce was the starting-rope withdrawn, when there
> Ladas stood crowned, yet had not turned a hair."

A parody upon this appeared upon a runner who was so slow that he seemed never to move:—

> "If Pericles there ran or sate, none know:
> He was so demoniacally slow.
> Scarce was the starting-rope withdrawn, when there
> Ladas stood crowned, and Pericles was—where?"

The serious epigram upon Ladas may be thus translated nearly as Hay has done:—

> "Such as thou wert when with aerial bound,
> Thy tiptoe never seen to touch the ground,
> Thou fledst, outstripping Thymus' swift career,—
> Such, Ladas, Myro's brass reveals thee here,
> Where every limb and sinew seems to breathe
> Assured prediction of the Pisan wreath."

It has been thought that the original epigram stopped here; but as given in the Anthology of Planudes there are four more lines, which perhaps rather weaken than improve the previous part. These have been thus translated :—

"How full of hope! those hollow flanks aspire
 To send up to the lips a breath-like fire.
 Soon on the wreath, unchecked, the brass will start,
 Oh, swifter than the wind, the sculptor's art!"

We formerly referred to Lysippus, the Court sculptor to Alexander the Great; and an epigram may here be given on a statue by him of that monarch, which was considered remarkable for its fidelity :—

On a Statue by Lysippus of Alexander the Great.
By Archelaus.

"Lysippus formed in brass the courage high
 Of Alexander, and his aspect bold :
 The brass looks up to heaven, and seems to cry :
 The earth is mine : thou, Jove, Olympus hold."

There are epigrams upon pictures of private persons, which are interesting—one in particular, by Nossis, a Locrian lady, on her child's picture; and another on a friend. The translations are by Hay :—

I.

"This is Melinna's self : the gentle child
 Looks sweetly on me with those eyes so mild.
 My own dear daughter—oh! what bliss to trace
 A parent's features in an infant face!"

II.

"Thymaretè, thy very self is there,
  Pictured in all thy dignity and grace:
Thy noble pride, thine awe-commanding air,
  Mingled with mildness in that lovely face;
Shaking his tail, thy faithful dog draws near,
Deeming he gazes on his mistress dear."

Another of the same kind is by Erinna:—

"This painting, best Prometheus, for thy shrine
Accept: see, human hands have skill like thine.
If he who thus this maiden drew had known
To add a voice, we had rejoiced to own
All Agatharchis to the life here shown."

Here is an epigram which obviously attempts to describe a picture mentioned by Pliny as painted by a Theban painter, Aristides, of a mother mortally wounded in a siege, but still in her last agony suckling her child. It is by Æmilianus:—

"Suck, hapless babe, this breast while yet I live;
Draw the last drop thy mother e'er can give.
The foeman's sword has robbed me of my breath,
But a true mother's love survives in death."

Some epigrams may here be added alluding to actual gems or other works of art of a minor character. Pliny tells us of a Satyr represented on a cup, rather put to sleep there than carved: an epigram embodies that very idea:—

"This Satyr was not carved, but laid asleep:
Nudge him, he'll wake in wrath; so, quiet keep."

Here is a description of a painting imitated on a crystal, the artist being Satyreius:—

> "Zeuxis' sweet colouring and style are here;
> In this small crystal all the charms appear
> Of great Arsinoe's form; you see her stand
> Fashioned and sent by Satyreius' hand;
> The likeness of the queenly dame am I,
> And noway short in grace or majesty."

Here is another epigram, describing a carved stone:—

> "A tiny stone, a jasper, here displays
> Five oxen carved, who seem to live and graze;
> And soon the little herd would wander hence,
> If not imprisoned by their golden fence."

Some of the epigrams of this artistic character may seem trifling, but others are undoubtedly fine, and all of them are interesting. Yet we venture to say that never was poetry in its best days employed to illustrate art with so much truth and beauty as in our own time, in Byron's exquisite description of the Dying Gladiator.

CHAPTER VII.

WITTY AND SATIRICAL.

It would not have been conformable either to human nature in general, or to Greek nature in particular, if the country and the literature that produced Aristophanes should not in its less serious compositions have given some place for wit and sarcasm. We find, accordingly, that these elements are not wanting. A great many epigrams both of a jocular and of a satirical kind are well deserving of notice, of which specimens shall now be given.

Nowhere, perhaps, are the proper objects of ridicule better set forth than in the Introduction to one of Foote's farces. He refuses to bring on the stage mere bodily defects or natural misfortunes; and when asked to say at what things we may laugh with propriety, answers thus:—" At an old beau, a superannuated beauty, a military coward, a stuttering orator, or a gouty dancer. In short, whoever affects to be what he is not, or strives to be what he cannot, is an object worthy the poet's pen and your mirth."

We do not say that the Greek epigrammatist always abstained from making merry at mere bodily defects; but we shall avoid as much as possible those that have no other recommendation. The proper object of ridicule is surely Folly, and the proper object of satire, Vice. Within the present section, however, will be included not merely the ridicule of sarcasm and the attacks of satire, but any also of those merry or witty views of nature and things that tend to produce sympathetic laughter.

Of bodily peculiarities there are some at which it is difficult not to smile; and if it is done good-humouredly, and rather as a warning to abstain from vanity or conceit, there is no harm in it. Many of such epigrams were probably written upon merely imaginary persons:—

A New Use of a Human Face.
Attributed to the Emperor Trajan: the translation old.

"With nose so long and mouth so wide,
And those twelve grinders side by side,
Dick, with a very little trial,
Would make an excellent sun-dial."

Some of the critics are greatly delighted to find that in this epigram the Emperor's knowledge of Greek was not such as to prevent him committing a false quantity.

A Counterpart to Narcissus.
By Lucillius: translated by Cowper.

"Beware, my friend! of crystal brook
Or fountain, lest that hideous hook,
　Thy nose, thou chance to see;
Narcissus' fate would then be thine,
And self-detested thou wouldst pine,
　As self-enamoured he."

Long and Short.
Anonymous: translated by Merivale.

"Dick cannot blow his nose whene'er he pleases,
   His nose so long is, and his arm so short;
Nor ever cries, God bless me! when he sneezes—
   He cannot hear so distant a report."

A variety of trades and professions have been traditional objects of ridicule. Schoolmasters and professors come in for their share.

On a Schoolmaster who had a Gay Wife.
By Lucillius.

"You in your school for ever flog and flay us,
   Teaching what Paris did to Menelaüs;
But all the while, within your private dwelling,
   There's many a Paris courting of your Helen."

On a Professor who had a Small Class.

"Hail, Aristides, Rhetoric's great professor!
Of wondrous words we own thee the possessor.
Hail ye, his pupils seven, that mutely hear him—
His room's four walls, and the three benches near him!"

This that follows is on Cadmus, without whom there might have been no grammar and little rhetoric. It is said to be by Zeno—not the philosopher, we presume. We give first a translation by Wellesley:—

"Take it not ill that Cadmus, Phœnician though he be,
Can say that Greece was taught by him to write her A, B, C."

This is good; but even "English readers" may know that A, B, C, is not the right name of the Greek alphabet. Let us respectfully propose a slight change:—

"Cadmus am I: then grudge me not the boast, that, though
   I am a
Phœnician born, I taught you Greeks your Alpha, Beta,
   Gamma."

The medical profession as usual comes in for some of those touches which we are ready enough to give or to enjoy when we are not actually in their hands.

A Convenient Partnership.
Anonymous.

"Damon, who plied the Undertaker's trade,
  With Doctor Crateas an agreement made.
  What linens Damon from the dead could seize,
  He to the Doctor sent for bandages;
  While the good Doctor, here no promise-breaker,
  Sent all his patients to the Undertaker."

Grammar and Medicine.
By Agathias.

" A thriving doctor sent his son to school
  To gain some knowledge, should he prove no fool ;
  But took him soon away with little warning,
  On finding out the lesson he was learning—
  How great Pelides' wrath, in Homer's rhyme,
  Sent many souls to Hades ere their time.
  ' No need for this my boy should hither come;
  That lesson he can better learn at home—
  For I myself, now, I make bold to say,
  Send many souls to Hades ere their day,
  Nor e'er find want of Grammar stop my way.'"

Musical attempts, when unsuccessful, are a fruitful and fair subject of ridicule. The following is by Nicarchus :—

"Men die when the night raven sings or cries:
But when Dick sings, e'en the night raven dies."

COMPENSATION.
By Leonidas.

"The harper Simylus, the whole night through,
Harped till his music all the neighbours slew:
All but deaf Origen, for whose dull *ears*
Nature atoned by giving length of *years*."

THE MUSICAL DOCTOR.
By Ammian: the translation altered from Wellesley.

"Nicias, a doctor and musician,
Lies under very foul suspicion.
He sings, and without any shame
He murders all the finest music:
Does he prescribe? our fate's the same,
If he shall e'er find me or you sick."

Unsuccessful painters, too, are sneered at. This is by Lucillius:—

"Eutychus many portraits made, and many sons begot;
But, strange to say! none ever saw a likeness in the lot."

Compliments to the fair sex are often paid by the epigrammatists in a manner at once witty and graceful.

We have seen how Sappho was described as a tenth Muse; but this epigram by an unknown author goes further. The translation is old and anonymous, though borrowed apparently from one by Swift, on which it has improved. It has been slightly altered:—

"The world must now two Venus's adore ;
Ten are the Muses, and the Graces four.
Such Dora's wit, so fair her form and face,
She's a new Muse, a Venus, and a Grace."

We find an adaptation of this to an accomplished Cornish lady, in an old magazine :—

"Now the Graces are four and the Venus's two,
  And ten is the number of Muses ;
For a Muse and a Grace and a Venus are you,
  My dear little Molly Trefusis."

Finally, we have another edition of this idea with a bit of satire at the end, which has been maliciously added by the translator :—

"Of Graces four, of Muses ten,
  Of Venus's now two are seen ;
Doris shines forth to dazzled men,
  A Grace, a Muse, and Beauty's Queen ;—
But let me whisper one thing more ;
The Furies now are likewise four."

The faults and foibles of women, springing often so naturally from their innate wish to please, have not escaped such of the epigrammatists as were inclined to satire, and some of them are bitter enough. The first we give must have been occasioned by some irritating disappointment, or have sprung from an unworthy opinion of the sex. It is by our friend Palladas :—

"All wives are plagues ; yet two blest times have they,—
Their bridal first, and then their burial day."

The others we give are less sweeping, and more

directed against individual failings, particularly the desire to appear more beautiful or more youthful than the facts warranted. This is by Lucillius:—

> "Chloe, those locks of raven hair,—
>   Some people say you dye them black;
> But that's a libel, I can swear,
>   For I know where you buy them black."

Our next deals with a very systematic dyer and getter-up of artificial juvenility, who seems to have been her own Madame Rachel. The Greek is Lucian's, and the translation by Merivale. There is also one by Cowper, which will be found among his works:—

> "Yes, you may dye your hair, but not your age,
>   Nor smooth, alas! the wrinkles of your face:
> Yes, you may varnish o'er the tell-tale page,
>   And wear a mask for every vanished grace.
> But there's an end. No Hecuba, by aid
> Of rouge and ceruse, is a Helen made."

The inactive habits of most of the Greek women are thought to have created a temptation to the use of these artificial modes of heightening the complexion, which would have been better effected by the natural pigments laid on by fresh air and exercise.

This is upon an old woman wishing to be married at rather an advanced period of life, by Nicarchus:—

> "Niconoë has doubtless reached her prime:
> Yes, for she did so in Deucalion's time.
> We don't know as to that, but think her doom
> Less fitted for a husband than a tomb."

This also is upon an old, or at least a plain woman, by Lucillius:—

"Gellia, your mirror's false; you could not bear,
If it were true, to see your image there."

On a Woman scornful in Youth playing the Coquette when Old.
By Rufinus.

"You now salute me graciously, when gone
Your beauty's power, that once like marble shone;
You now look sweet, though forced to hide away
Those locks that o'er your proud neck used to stray.
Vain are your arts: your faded charms I scorn;
The rose now past, I care not for the thorn."

Upon a Lady's coy, reluctant, "unamorous" Delay.
By Rufinus.

"How long, hard Prodicè, am I to kneel,
And pray and whine, to move that breast of steel?
You e'en are getting grey, as much as I am;
We soon shall be—just Hecuba and Priam."

Deafness is an infirmity which is a proper object, not of ridicule, but of pity; but then the deaf person should not pretend to hear when he or she cannot, as was the case with the old lady now to be noticed:—

On a Deaf Housekeeper.
(Paraphrased.)

"Of all life's plagues I recommend to no man
To hire as a domestic a deaf woman.
I've got one who my orders does not hear,
Mishears them rather, and keeps blundering near.

Thirsty and hot, I asked her for a *drink;*
She bustled out, and brought me back some *ink.*
Eating a good rump-steak, I called for *mustard;*
Away she went, and whipped me up a *custard.*
I wanted with my chicken to have *ham;*
Blundering once more, she brought a pot of *jam.*
I wished in season for a cut of *salmon,*
And what she bought me was a huge fat *gammon.*
I can't my voice raise higher and still higher,
As if I were a herald or town-crier.
'Twould better be if she were deaf outright;
But anyhow she quits my house this night."

Those ladies—generally, of course, such as were advanced in life—who unblushingly betook themselves to the bottle, are an inevitable subject of satire. It has already been mentioned that even men were considered intemperate who drank wine without a large admixture of water; but apparently the female topers, having once broken bounds, took their wine unmixed.

Epitaph on Maronis.

"This rudely sculptured Cup will show
　Where grey Maronis lies below.
She talked, and drank strong unmixed stuff,
　Both of them more than *quantum suff.*
She does not for her children grieve,
　Nor their poor father grudge to leave;
　　It only vexes her to think
　　This drinking-cup's not filled with drink."

The last couplet might be more literally translated thus:—

"But in the grave she scarcely can lie still,
To think, what Bacchus owns, she can't with Bacchus fill."

Love is sometimes treated of in a vein of pleasantry, very different from the deep and impassioned tone in which it is exhibited in more serious compositions. Take some examples:—

Is a *BLACK* Woman one of the *FAIR* Sex?
By Meleager.

"By Didyma's beauty I'm carried away;
I melt, when I see it, like wax before fire:
She is black, it is true: so are coals; but even they,
When they're warmed, a bright glow like the rose-cup
    acquire."

This is by Archias, Cicero's friend and client, written perhaps to illustrate some piece of art:—

"What! fly from love? vain hope: there's no retreat,
    When he has wings and I have only feet."

This is by Crates, translated by Sayers, Southey's friend:—

Cures for Love.

"Hunger, perhaps, may cure your love,
  Or time your passion greatly alter:
If both should unsuccessful prove,
  I strongly recommend a halter."

Venus and the Muses.
By some said to be Plato's.

"To the Muses said Venus: 'Maids, mind what you do;
Honour me, or I'll set my boy Cupid on you.'
Then to Venus the Muses: 'To Mars chatter thus:
Your urchin ne'er ventures to fly upon us.'"

The light and cheerful way in which poor men speak of their poverty is often pleasant. Here are some examples:—

WANT A GOOD WATCH-DOG.
By Julian: the translation by Wellesley.

"Seek a more profitable job,
  Good housebreakers, elsewhere:
These premises you cannot rob,
  Want guards them with such care."

THE POOR SCHOLAR'S ADMONITION TO THE MICE.
By Aristo.

"O mice! if here you come for food, you'd better go elsewhere,
For in this cabin, small and rude, you'll find but slender fare.
Go where you'll meet with good fat cheese, and sweet dried figs in plenty,
Where even the scraps will yield with ease a banquet rich and dainty:
If to devour my books you come, you'll rue it, without question,
And find them all, as I find some, of very hard digestion."

The folly of fools is a fair subject of ridicule. This is by Lucian:—

"A blockhead bit by fleas put out the light,
And chuckling cried, Now you can't see to bite."

Here is something which the Greeks considered folly, by Lucian:—

"While others tippled, Sam from drinking shrunk,
Which made the rest think Sam alone was drunk."

Without recommending excess, there are a good many invitations to jollity. Here is one :—

"Sober Eubulus, friends, lies here below:
So then, let's drink : to Hades all must go."

What follows is a favourite sentiment—perhaps too much so—with the old poets :—

"Wine to the poet is a wingèd steed ;
Those who drink water come but little speed."

One great poet has existed in our day who was a signal exception to this alleged rule.

The following is by the Emperor Julian, and refers to that substitute for wine which the Germans discovered by fermenting, or, as Tacitus calls it, *corrupting*, grain. It does not seem to have pleased the imperial wine-drinker. The translation is necessarily paraphrastic :—

"Who ? whence this, Bacchus ? for by Bacchus' self,
The son of Jove, I know not this strange elf.
The other smells like nectar : but thou here
Like the he-goat. Those wretched Kelts, I fear,
For want of grapes made thee of ears of corn.
Demetrius art thou, of Demeter born,
Not Bacchus, Dionysus, nor yet wine—
Those names but fit the products of the vine ;
BEER thou mayst be from Barley; or, that failing,
We'll call thee ALE, for thou wilt keep us ailing."

A bath to the Greeks, as we might expect—at least, in their later development—was a great enjoyment, if not a necessity of life. The epigrammatists supply us with many pleasant and playful inscriptions for baths or bathing-places, illustrating their virtues and attractions. The purity and freshness of the water are natural themes of eulogium, and the patronage of divine beings is readily supposed. Here is a selection, all of them apparently anonymous :—

"This bath may boast the Graces' own to be,—
And for that reason it holds only three."

"Here bathed the Graces, and at leaving gave
Their choicest splendours to requite the wave."

Or thus, which we may suppose written of the draped Graces :—

"Here bathed the Graces, and, by way of payment,
Left half their charms when they resumed their raiment."

"Here Venus bathed, ere she to Paris' eyes
Displayed the immortal form that gained the prize."

Or thus :—

"Straight from this bath went Venus, wet and dripping;
To Paris showed herself—and won the pippin."

"Either these waves gave Venus birth, or she,
Her form here bathing, made them what we see."

ON A SMALL-SIZED BATH.

"Blame not things little : Grace may on them wait.
Cupid is little; but his godhead's great."

We are warned, however, that excess in the use of the warm bath, as in other indulgences, may be injurious :—

"Wine and the bath, and lawless love for ladies,
  Just send us quicker down the hill to Hades."

Some vices are particularly obnoxious to the satirical epigrammatist, especially avarice and envy:—

STINGINESS IN HOSPITALITY.

By Pallas: translation altered from Wellesley.

"Most people dine but once, but when we've dined
    With our friend Salaminus,
We dine again at home, for faith! we find
    He did not truly dine us."

BOARD OR LODGING.

By Lucillius: translation altered from Cowper.

"Asclépiades, the Miser, in his house
Espied one day, with some surprise, a mouse:
'Tell me, dear mouse,' he cried, 'to what cause is it
I owe this pleasant but unlooked-for visit?'
The mouse said, smiling: 'Fear not for your hoard:
I come, my friend, to lodge, and not to board.'"

There are several vigorous denunciations of the vice of envy. This is anonymous:—

"Envy is vile, but plays a useful part,
  Torturing in envious men both eyes and heart."

This is in that exaggerated style which the epigrams sometimes exhibit. It is by Lucillius — the translation from Wellesley:—

"Poor Diophon of envy died,
  His brother thief to see
Nailed near him, to be crucified,
  Upon a higher tree."

But the best epigram on this subject is to be found in one which seems to describe a picture of Momus the fault-finder, the impersonation of Envy, perhaps also, some will say, of Criticism,—the Power who could produce nothing excellent himself, and who never saw unmixed excellence in the works of others. The picture is supposed to have been by Apelles. The epigram is anonymous; the translation partly from Hay:—

" Who here has formed, with faultless hand and skill,
Fault-finding Momus, source of endless ill ?
On the bare earth his aged limbs are thrown,
As if in life, to lie and sigh and groan.
His frame is wasted, and his scanty hairs
One trembling hand from his thin temple tears:
With his old staff the other strikes the ground,
Which all insensate to the blows is found.
In double row his gnashing teeth declare
How much his neighbour's weal o'erwhelms him with
    despair."

Swift made a well-known epitaph upon Vanbrugh as an architect :—

" Lie heavy on him, earth, for he
  Laid many a heavy load on thee."

This is nearly the counterpart of the following Greek epigram :—

"Hail, Mother Earth ! lie light on him
  Whose tombstone here we see :
Æsigenes, his form was slim,
  And light his weight on thee."

A similar request is made in another epigram by Am

mianus, but with a very different feeling. The translation is by Merivale:—

> "Light lie the earth, Nearchus, on thy clay,—
> That so the dogs may easier find their prey."

This anonymous epigram is upon a matricide, who does not deserve burial:—

> "Bury him not! no burial is for him:
> Let hungry dogs devour him limb by limb.
> Our general Mother, Earth, on her kind breast
> Will ne'er allow a matricide to rest."

The satirical epigrammatists indulge often in national invective, and indeed the Greeks were too fond of abusing some of their neighbours. Here are specimens:—

> "A viper bit a Cappadocian's hide;
> But 'twas the viper, not the man, that died."

The natives of many other countries besides Cappadocia were called *bad:* among the rest the Lerians; thus:—

> "Lerians are bad: not *some* bad, and some *not;*
> But all; there's not a Lerian in the lot,
> Save Procles, that you could a good man call;—
> And Procles—is a Lerian after all."

Our readers will here recognise the original of a well-known epigram by Porson, which exists both in a Greek and English shape, and where the satirist, after denouncing the Germans as *all* ignorant of Greek metres, concludes:—

"All, save only Hermann;—
And Hermann's a German."

It was unfortunate for poor Hermann that his name and his nationality rhymed so well together.

An epigram may here be given in conclusion on this head, as tending, perhaps, to illustrate the transition by which the satirical Greek epigram came to resemble the favourite style of Martial which has been so much adopted in modern times.

The epigram we refer to is by Lucillius:—

On a Declamatory Pleader.

"A little pig, an ox, a goat (my only one), I lost,
And Menecles, to plead my cause, I fee'd at some small cost.
I only wanted back my beasts, which seemed my simple due;
Then, Menecles, what had I with Othryades to do?
I never thought in this affair to charge with any theft
The men who, at Thermopylæ, their lives and bodies left.
My suit is with Eutychides; and if I get decree,
Leonidas and Xerxes both are welcome to go free.
Plead my true case: lest I cry out (I can't my feelings smother),
'The little pig one story tells, and Menecles another.'"

This satire upon a certain class of lawyers agrees completely with an epigram of Martial's; and as Lucillius and he lived nearly about the same time, it would be interesting to know if the one was borrowed from the other, and which. The preponderance of evidence rather is that Lucillius, as Lessing thinks, was a century, or at least half a century, later than Martial, and is probably, therefore, the imitator in this matter, though his imitation is not slavish. Martial's epigram has been translated into French by La Monnoye.

This chapter may be concluded with a mild satire upon the condition of the times, with reference to the two ancient worthies, Heraclitus and Democritus, the weeping and the laughing philosopher. The translation is mainly from Prior:—

" Sad Heraclitus, with thy tears return;
Life more than ever gives us cause to mourn.
Democritus, dear droll, revisit earth :
Life more than ever gives us cause for mirth.
Between you both I stand in thoughtful pother,
How I should weep with one, how laugh with t'other."

CHAPTER VIII.

NARRATIVE AND MISCELLANEOUS.

The concluding chapter of our volume will consist of Narrative epigrams and some others of a miscellaneous kind, not easily reducible to other heads. No systematic order can well be observed in a congeries of this kind; but it may begin with those that are shortest and simplest.

The first that occurs is well known as a curiosity, and as an exercise for translators in the power of condensation and equipoise. The original consists of two lines, and any expansion of it must be looked on as an evasion of the difficulty.

The Contrast.

"One finding gold, left there a rope; but he who in the ground
Had left the gold, not finding it, put on the rope he found."

The above epigram is said to be by Plato, but not probably the philosopher. The next is attributed to Antiphilus:—

"Deficient one in limbs, and one in eyes,
Each with the other's help his want supplies:

> The blind man lifts the lame man on his back,
> And by the other's words directs his track.
> Wholesome necessity this lesson taught,—
> By mutual pity, mutual aid was brought."

This shorter one, on the same subject, bears the name of Plato the younger:—

> "The blind man bears the lame, and onward hies,
> Made right by lending feet and borrowing eyes."

The next that comes has always been a favourite, and has been translated by several modern Latin poets. The original is anonymous:—

> "Young, I was poor; now rich in my old age,
> My lot each way your pity may engage.
> Wealth, when I could enjoy it, I had none;
> Now that I have it, the enjoyment's gone."

To which an Englishman has ventured on this reply:—

> "Come, friend; methinks your fate in either season,
> For such complaints affords but slender reason.
> Youth, when with vigour joined, requires no wealth;
> It finds its happiness in hope and health:
> While age, tho' torpid, has the power to take
> Pleasure in money for its own mere sake;
> Or if a nobler feeling warms the breast,
> Is happy thereby to make others blest."

The next is given as an example of what the Greeks called *storgè*, or parental affection in the animal world. The original is by Alphèus. The version is partly from Hay and partly from Sir A. Croke, in Wellesley:—

> "Covered with wintry snows, around her young,
> With sheltering wings, a fond hen-mother clung,

Till by heaven's frosts she perished; to the last
Struggling against the skies and bitter blast.
Prognè, Medea, ye were mothers too;
In Hades blush—to learn what birds can do."

This that follows is a story by Anytè upon three Milesian ladies, who, when their city was invaded by the Gauls, escaped by self-destruction from the insults offered to them; the translation by Merivale:—

"Then let us hence, Miletus dear; sweet native land, farewell;
Th' insulting wrongs of lawless Gauls we fear, whilst here we dwell.
Three virgins of Milesian race, to this dire fate compell'd
By Celtic Mars—yet glad we die, that we have ne'er beheld
'Spousals of blood, nor sunk to be vile handmaids to our foes,
But rather owe our thanks to Death, kind healer of our woes."

There are two epigrams on a child being saved from destruction by its mother's presence of mind. We give one of these, by Parmenio:—

"Her child once leaning o'er the extreme roof
Of a high house (children are free from fear),
Its mother bared her breast, yet kept aloof,
And made her child to its loved haunt draw near:
Thus did the milky fount, in that blest hour
Of giving life, exert a double power."

There is another epigram on this subject, but it is unnecessary to insert it, as the main idea is the same, and it is chiefly distinguished by referring to the fate of Astyanax, the son of Hector, who was thrown by the Greeks from a high place and killed. Rogers the poet has imitated these epigrams in some well-known lines:—

> "While on the cliff with calm delight she kneels,
> And the blue vales a thousand joys recall,
> See, to the last, last verge her infant steals!
> O fly, yet stir not, speak not, lest it fall!
> Far better taught, she lays her bosom bare,
> And the fond boy springs back to nestle there."

The following story is told of a skilful diver who did good service to the Greeks during the Persian war by conveying information to them without being detected, and who is said to have approached under water the Persian galleys, when anchored near the Greek coast, and to have cut the cables, so as to expose the vessels to a violent storm. He was employed in these services by Themistocles, to which fact the epigram makes reference:—

> "When Xerxes poured on Greece his rabble rout,
> Skyllus a warfare 'neath the wave found out;
> Diving where ships had hoped a safe retreat,
> He cut the cables of the anchored fleet:
> Persia and all her crews, thus driven to land,
> Staggered, and prostrate lay upon the strand,
> The first-fruits of Themistocles' command."

IBYCUS AND THE CRANES.

> "Ibycus, bent the desert to explore,
> There robbers slew thee, on the lonely shore;
> Thy cries brought down a passing flock of cranes,
> Who came and witnessed thy last dying pains;—
> And not in vain. A Fury, ire-inflamed,
> Avenged thy death, which those good birds proclaimed,

On Corinth's ground. By greed of lucre driven,
Ye robbers, fear ye not the wrath of Heaven?
Ægysthus, when he doomed a Bard to die,
Did not escape the black-robed Fury's eye."

The story just given is well known, from its being the subject of a poem of Schiller's. The last couplet alludes to an act of Ægysthus in putting to death a bard, a friend of Agamemnon's, who was observing and endeavouring to restrain Clytemnestra's conduct.

Here is a rather marvellous story of a crow; but it appears to have the authority of Pliny in its favour. It is by Bianor:—

"The bird of Phœbus, parched with thirst's dire pain,
A housewife's pitcher spied, for catching rain:
He perched, loud croaking, on the brim, but no,—
Too short his beak, the water much too low!
Thy power then, Phœbus, in the bird inspired
An artifice to gain what he desired:
With gathered pebbles, quickly to the brink
He raised the water's level, and could drink."

The Draught-Ox.
By Addœus.

"The old draught-ox, worn in the furrowed field,
Alcon to ruthless slaughter would not yield,
His toils revering: in deep pasture now
He lows, and feels his freedom from the plough."

It was a religious scruple with the ancient Greeks not to sacrifice a plough-ox.

The story that follows—for it is a story, though it concludes with a precept—is an illustration of that power of Nemesis which has been referred to in another part of this volume, and it is directed against the presumptuousness of doing what is sometimes called fore-speaking Providence :—

> "My gallant ship now nears my native shore;
> *To-morrow!* and her stormy course is o'er.
> To-morrow!—when my lips these words had said,
> A sea like Hades, raving o'er my head,
> Engulphed me; and destruction round me clung,
> For this vain vaunting of a froward tongue.
> Say not *to-morrow;* the tongue's slightest slip
> Nemesis watches, ere it pass the lip."

The epigram is by Antiphilus, the translation by Hay, slightly altered.

A wayside nut-tree here complains of the schoolboys. It is by Antipater, or, as some say, Plato :—

> "A roadside nut-tree planted, here I stand,
> A mark for every passing schoolboy's hand;
> My boughs and flourishing twigs all broke or bent—
> Wounded by many a missile at me sent.
> What boots it now that trees should fruitful be ?—
> My very fruit brings this disgrace on me!"

The next is rather an old-fashioned story, told of Pittacus, one of the Seven sages :—

> "An Atarnean stranger once to Pittacus applied,
> That ancient sage, Hyrradius' son, and Mitylene's pride:
> 'Grave sir, betwixt two marriages I now have power to choose,
> And hope you will advise me which to take and which refuse.
> One of the maidens, every way, is very near myself;
> The other's far above me, both in pedigree and pelf.

Now which is best ?'   The old man raised the staff which
    old men bear,
And with it pointed to some boys that then were playing
    there,
Whipping their tops along the street : ' Their steps,' he
    said, ' pursue,
And look, and listen carefully ; they'll tell you what to do.'
Following them, the stranger went to see what might befall,
And 'Whip the top that's nearest you !' was still their
    constant call.
He, by this boyish lesson taught, resigned the high-born
    dame,
And wed the maiden 'nearest him.' Go thou and do the
    same !"

The story that follows is of a he-goat, but it is connected with circumstances of a curious and interesting kind. It is made the vehicle of recording the religious custom by which the Goat, from its habit of devouring the branches of the vine, was held obnoxious to Bacchus, and sacrificed to him accordingly. It may be mentioned that the word Tragedy means literally a goat-song, such as was sung or repeated at these sacrifices to Bacchus. The epigram is by Leonidas of Tarentum, but it seems to have been imitated or abridged by Evenus, of whose composition a single couplet only remains. Leonidas's epigram may be thus translated :—

" The she-goat's bounding and well-bearded spouse,
  On the vine's tender shoots intent to browse,
  A Voice from earth addressed—' Vile wretch, devour
  Our fruitful twigs, for short-lived is your power !
  This firm root soon will nectar yield again,
  To pour on you, he-goat, when at the altar slain.' "

The couplet preserved of Evenus's composition, and which Ovid copied, may be turned into this quatrain:—

"Though you should gnaw me to the root,
   Yet, he-goat, to the altar led,
You'll find I've borne enough of fruit
   To pour on your devoted head."

This composition attained in the reign of Domitian a celebrity and importance worth recording. That emperor, whose character exhibited a strange mixture of good and evil, explicable only on the supposition of his insanity, issued an edict to prohibit the cultivation of vineyards—at least, without an imperial licence. He seems to have thought that vine-culture interfered with the cultivation of corn, and may have wished to obviate mischief produced among some of his soldiers by intemperance. But the wine-growers naturally were indignant; and being no doubt as much alive to their own interests as the licensed victuallers of the present day, they set themselves to procure the recall of the edict, which they effected partly by the dissemination of what Mr Merivale calls an ominous parody on this epigram, in which the name of Cæsar was substituted for that of he-goat. Domitian probably was superstitious enough to think that by destroying the vines he was becoming, like the he-goat, obnoxious to Bacchus, and might fall a sacrifice to the god's displeasure or to the resentment of his votaries, of which there were not wanting examples in mythological history.

Here are two deathbed scenes, expressed, we think, with a touching degree of pathos:—

"These her last words the weeping Gorgo said,
  As round her mother's neck her hands she laid:
  'Stay with my father, and a daughter bear,
  Who may, with happier fate, of thy grey age have care.'"

"Holding her father in a last embrace,
  Erato spoke, while tears bedewed her face:
  'Father, I am no more; death clouds my eye
  Even now, with its black shadow, while I die.'"

The following, by Palladas, gives a striking picture of a heathen's views of Divine Providence,—for the author is thought not to have been a Christian, or if he was, he may have written the verses in a heathen character. Sarapis, or, as it is sometimes written, Serapis, was, as we are told, an Egyptian divinity, whose worship was introduced into Greece in the time of the Ptolemys. He was held in great veneration at Alexandria, to which place Palladas belonged, and it has been said that this is the name given to Apis after his death and deification. Serapis corresponds to the Greek Jupiter and Pluto united, and his image is often to be seen on works of art, with the peculiar attribute of a *modius* or corn-measure on his head. The version is Hay's, slightly altered :—

"Serapis to a murderer, they say,
  Came in a vision, while asleep he lay,
  Near a frail wall,—and thus his dictate ran :
  'Up, go, sleep elsewhere, thou most wretched man !'
  He, startled, changed his place, when, hark ! that sound :
  With sudden crash the wall comes to the ground.
  With joy the wretch an offering soon provides,
  Thinking the god is pleased with homicides.

But now again that voice is heard by night :
'Think'st thou that I in men like thee delight ?
I saved thee once—it was a painless fate
Averted—but know this, my righteous hate
Reserved thee for the cross, whose pangs thy crimes
    await.' "

Here are two mutually contrasted stories, showing the return made by the gods for the opposite qualities of humane compassion and contemptuous insensibility in reference to the dead. It should be explained that it was thought by the ancients a stringent duty to bury the dead, or any part of a dead body left without sepulture. We may remember, also, that to " bury the dead " is one of the seven Corporal mercies of the Christian Church :—

" A dead man's skull, cast on the public road,
  A traveller saw, nor sign of pity showed ;
Lifting a stone, he threw it at the head,
  Nor feared for retribution from the dead.
But, back rebounding from the bone, its flight
  Quenched the unfeeling jester's power of sight.
Hereafter, too, he'll feel it, and lament
  The foolish skill that such a missile sent."

The author of the companion story is Carphyllides, and the version we give is Mr Hay's :—

" While from the strand his line a fisher threw,
  Shoreward a shipwrecked human head he drew.
His moistened eyes soft drops of pity shed,
  While gazing on the bald and trunkless head.
No spade he had ; but while his active hands
  Scraped a small grave among the yielding sands,
A store of gold, there hid, he found. Yes ! yes !
Heaven will the just man's pious actions bless."

The next story to be given is a very celebrated one. It is by Callimachus, expressed with his usual brevity and elegance. It is mentioned by Cicero, and translated by him from a text somewhat different, apparently, from what we possess. Two translations shall be given to help the illustration of it. The first is rather more literal than the second, which is by Mr Burgon, and given in Dr Wellesley's book :—

" Cleombrotus, the Ambraciote, having said—
' Thou sun, farewell !' leapt down among the dead
From the high wall : no sorrow had he known,
Nor was there cause for death, save this alone—
Plato upon the Soul, the ardent youth had read."

"'Farewell, thou sun !' Cleombrotus, the bold Ambraciote, cried,
And hurled himself, impetuous, from the lofty rampart's side ;
Yet nought there was on all the earth to urge him to the deed,
Save Plato's matchless ' Phædon,' which 'twas known he loved to read."

The motive of this act has been the subject of speculation—whether it was curiosity, or perplexity, or a sense of the comparative vanity of earthly things. The quality of the act, too, was discussed among the Fathers of the Church, and different opinions expressed. In a ludicrous epigram by Agathias upon a Sophist who was questioned as to the nature of the soul, and who answered in very vague terms, the conclusion of his answer is :—

> "If more you wish to learn, to Hades go,
> And there as much as Plato soon you'll know.
> Or if you choose, ascend the rampart's height,
> Mimic Cleombrotus, and plunge to-night:
> The soul, thus without body left alone,
> May have the truth it seeks for clearly shown,—
> If there's indeed a soul, to know, or to be known."

WHAT WORDS HECTOR WOULD HAVE SAID IF STRUCK BY THE GREEKS AFTER HE WAS DEAD.

Anonymous.

> "Wound now my lifeless form; ev'n hares exult
> O'er the fall'n lion, and his corse insult."

Instead of a story we may give here a supposed address of Troy to Minerva on the goddess deserting her, by Agathias :—

> "Guardian of Troy relent: I thee adore
> Still in my misery as I did before.
> But thou hast given me to the foe a prey:
> All for an apple, must my bliss give way!
> The Shepherd's death might have sufficed: if He
> Unjustly judged, yet Troy from blame was free."

As a counterpart of this epigram, another shall be given, ascribed to the Emperor Hadrian, upon the resuscitation of Troy under the Roman power. The translation is by Goldwin Smith :—

> "Hector, brave heart, if still thy spirit hears,
> O list, and stay awhile thy patriot tears!
> Troy stands a noble city; and in war
> Her sons, though weak to thee, still valiant are.
> The Myrmidons are gone. To Achilles say,
> Æneas' offspring all Thessalia sway."

As a further form of retribution against Greece may

be given the lament for the destruction of Corinth by the Romans, the supposed descendants of Troy. The epigram is by Antipater, the translation by Wellesley:—

"Where are thy splendours, Dorian Corinth, where
  Thy crested turrets, thy ancestral goods,
The temples of the blest, the dwellings fair,
  The high-born dames, the myriad multitudes?
There's not a trace of thee, sad doomed one, left,
By rav'ning war at once of all bereft.
We, the sad Nereids, offspring of the surge,
Alone are spared to chant thy halcyon dirge."

We give another on the same subject by Polystratus, translated by Charles Merivale, as more clearly bringing out the supposed retribution to which we have referred. The destruction of Corinth by Mummius was a signally important event both to Greece and Rome. It reduced that profligate city to desolation for a century and a half, though in St Paul's time her prosperity as well as her profligacy had revived. But in reference to Rome, the taking of Corinth led to the introduction of that taste for Art of which the Romans had previously been destitute. Mummius was so ignorant of the very conception of excellence in Art that the main precaution he took in having pictures and statues conveyed to Rome was to stipulate that in the case of their injury or destruction, the parties intrusted with them should replace them with new ones.

"Achæan Acrocorinth, the bright star
  Of Hellas, with its narrow Isthmian bound,
Lucius o'ercame, in one enormous mound
  Piling the dead, conspicuous from afar.

Thus, to the Greeks denying funeral fires,
  Have great Æneas' later progeny
  Performed high Jove's retributive decree,
And well avenged the city of their sires!"

The next that we give is a kind of story, embodied in the song of the Cretan warrior bearing the name of Hybrias. There are many good translations of this piece, but we prefer to give the version by Leyden, which we think deserves to be rescued from the oblivion with which it has been threatened:—

"My spear, my sword, my shaggy shield!
  With these I till, with these I sow;
With these I reap my harvest field,—
  No other wealth the gods bestow:
With these I plant the fertile vine;
With these I press the luscious wine.

My spear, my sword, my shaggy shield!
  They make me lord of all below,—
For those who dread my spear to wield,
  Before my shaggy shield must bow.
Their fields, their vineyards, they resign,
And all that cowards have is mine."

The chapter and the volume may be concluded with the anonymous motto which more than one adventurer is said to have adopted at the conclusion of their story:—

"Fortune and Hope, farewell! I've gained the port;
  You've fooled me long—make others now your sport."

APPENDIX.

SOME PRINCIPAL DATES CONNECTED WITH THE ANTHOLOGIES, AND THE ERAS OF SOME OF THE POETS WHOSE EPIGRAMS ARE INSERTED IN THEM.

Meleager's Garland, compiled in the end of the second century B.C.

Philippus's Collection, made about the end of the second century A.D.

In each of these collections, lists of the poets are given whose epigrams are contained in them; and by this means an approximation can be made to the dates at which they flourished.

Agathias's Collection, made in the sixth century A.D.

Eras of some of the more remarkable Poets:—

	B.C.
Archilochus,	687
Sappho, about	611
Simonides,	556 b. / 467 d.
Leonidas of Tarentum,	Middle of 3d century B.C.
Callimachus, about	256
Antipater of Sidon,	127
Meleager,	95
Nossis, Anytè (?), Erinna (?)	3d century B.C., but considerable uncertainty attending two of these poetesses.

THE END.

www.ingramcontent.com/pod-product-compliance
Lightning Source LLC
Chambersburg PA
CBHW020826230426
43666CB00007B/1116